RED LETTERS

A Jesus Devotional

PHILIP MONNIN

Table of Contents

INTRODUCTION

When Jesus shared with me what He wanted for this book, His instructions were to revisit His words from the pages of the New Testament. As I read each verse, I was struck by the timeless perfection of the truths they contained. I listened to Jesus and wrote down what He had to say in relation to each of them. I was both personally convicted of how far I have to go to live up to His words and saddened by how far we, His Church, have strayed from Him.

Following Jesus is supposed to be uncomplicated. It doesn't require an advanced theological degree or even a mastery of the Bible. Jesus asks only for the humble surrendering of our hearts to His will and a desire to learn His ways. He takes care of the rest. This is the way of a disciple.

Come along and see what Jesus has to say to you. It will truly change your life.

Philip Monnin   December 2019

JANUARY

Jesus asked many questions of those around
Him. These questions are deep and purposeful.
They bring clarity of heart by pointing to the
truth. And truth brings His freedom.

JANUARY 1

What are you seeking?

John 1:38

❧

I am the God of endless possibilities. I take the long view of your life lived for Me. I know My plans and what you will need to accomplish them.

What are you seeking? I ask this question of each of My children. The answer reveals the true desires of one's heart. Many seek after things that will pass away—momentary pleasures, or possessions, or changes in circumstances. I am a much greater God than this. I have bigger plans for you than these small requests. What I long for most is your heart. I want your desire to be for Me. This is why I created you—to walk with Me in deep fellowship. And when we do, you will discover that I already know what you truly need and will provide for you along the way.

What do you seek, My child? Take hold of My hand and let us walk. We will talk about it along the way.

January 2

What were you discussing on the way?

Mark 9:33

ॐॐ

You only know a portion of My plans for you. If I revealed them all, you could not bear the weight of their magnitude. The key is to walk one step at a time with Me, and let Me show you the next step.

Some make it a habit to try to figure out where we are going and how we will get there. They churn endlessly over the details in their minds even though we are only taking the next step. Their feet want to run away on the wings of their thoughts. But this is not My way. Instead, My way is the way of preparation. With your cooperation, I build your foundation day by day. We move together through the tests, trials, and triumphs that lead us toward the final destination, which is your destiny on earth.

Listen for My voice. Look for what I am already doing in your life. Do not get ahead of Me. We will get to where we are going and will arrive prepared for the tasks that await.

JANUARY 3

Whom do you seek?

John 18:4

૭૪૭

I am the light. Those who are seeking the light come to Me. My light is pure and untainted by the imaginations of man. There is no darkness in My light, only truth.

Many of My children want more than I am. They spend countless hours adding to My simple invitation and ways. Others want less of Me than I am. They cut away much of My richness and limit Me to what their minds can accept. This is how a golden calf is formed...a little more here, a little less there. Some polish and a little buffing. Soon, I am no longer the object of their worship but have been replaced by a god of their own making. Though I am a God beyond all you could think or imagine, yet I come to you on the simplest of terms. The words I have spoken to you bring life—abundant life without burdens. Golden calves are heavy. They are difficult to carry. They require much maintenance.

Do not try to change Me. I am already sufficient. Instead, get to know Me in all of My glorious facets. You do not need to remake Me in your image. I am who I am.

JANUARY 4

What do you think about the Christ?

Matthew 22:42

☙❧

It is true I can be known by My Word, but I give each of My children the opportunity to know Me personally. It can be a rich relationship where I give each one as much of Me as they desire.

I am interested in what you think about Me. I want you to know Me intimately as a husband and wife know each other. *Think on this for a moment.* Is a husband not aware of all his spouse has done for him? Is his wife not aware of the sacrifices made on her behalf? Is not all revealed in their intimacy? I know you in this way. I see every act as we walk together. I reach out to you as you stumble and steady you for the next step. I listen to the deep thoughts of your heart. I hold dear each and every tear.

Know Me in this same way. I came to earth for you. I lived for you. I died for you. I now live again so you can also live. My power searches for expression through your weakness. My love for you guides My every thought of you.

JANUARY 5

Who do the crowds say that I am?

Luke 9:18

❧

I defy the opinions of the crowds, though they are many. Each seeks to understand Me in their own way, but I can only be understood as I truly am.

I am who I am. These words spoken by Me so long ago to Moses from the midst of the burning branches stand as truth. The world seeks to twist and turn them—or even silence them, if it were possible. In this cacophony of false concepts being shouted ever and ever louder, you must stand against the flow of popular opinion and listen for the truth spoken quietly by Me into your heart. If you seek Me, you will find Me. But do not be surprised if I am more than you ever thought I would be.

Do not be conformed to the doctrines and traditions of those who seek to limit Me. I will show you who I am both by My Word and during our walk together. Stand on this truth! It is a firm place for your feet. You will not slip.

JANUARY 6

But who do you say that I am?

Luke 9:20

ॐॐ

Each person must answer this question. The response carries eternal consequences.

Who am I to you? As we walk along the way each day, what are your thoughts toward Me? The answers to these questions determine our relationship. Will this relationship be a close collaboration of shared purposes and desires? Or will it be defined by the arms-length distance of reluctance or indifference?

I am the Lord God Almighty. This is a fact. But I am your greatest admirer and a friend closer than any brother. I love you. I delight in your presence each day. I long for your love and devotion. I seek your cooperation in things great and small. I desire you to be one of My closest disciples. This is who I am.

JANUARY 7

Do you believe in the Son of Man?

John 9:35

❧❧

I am not a god of stone, wood, or any vain imagination. I am the God of all truth. I came for you so you could have an endless life filled with an abundance of Me.

I can be trusted. Believing *in* Me is more than believing *about* Me. It is the very act of trusting Me. Trust and faith go hand in hand. Where one is found, the other is not far away. Give Me even the smallest kernel of faith, and I will move the mountains out of your way. This works because I do all the heavy lifting while you trust and watch Me work. Many do not understand this. They think they need to help Me. I tell you that you cannot even believe in Me without the help of the Holy Spirit. So, whatever you face, whether it is great or small, come to Me with the faith you have, and ask Me to show you what to do. You will be amazed.

I desire to be your God in all things. I look to occupy the recesses of your heart. Do not keep anything from Me, My child. The more you trust Me, the more we will do *together*.

JANUARY 8

What do you want me to do for you?

Mark 10:36

࿊

What I do for you is done out of love. What I do not do for you is done out of this same love.

It is My great pleasure to give gifts to My children. However, not every request is for your benefit. Some can bring distance between us or delay the plans I have for you. It is important to understand there is more to asking than making a request. What you ask must align with My will for you. It must be made with pure motives. And you cannot ask that I overrule someone else's will. Many make these mistakes and ask amiss. They then become angry and discouraged, accusing Me of not listening or caring. Be assured, I hear your requests, and I care deeply for you. But remember that My actions are motivated by My pure love for you and nothing else.

Seek My will in all things. Then, when you ask, I will do it for you. Do not become discouraged if you must wait. I have all the time in the world. My timing for you is perfect.

JANUARY 9

Where are we to buy bread, so that these people may eat?

John 6:5

❧❧

The *impossible* is where I delight in working. It is that place beyond human capabilities where all is subject to My will.

I operate from a supernatural perspective. I am not bound by the concepts of time, space, or human ability. My realm is the miraculous. It is wrought in the midst of the weaknesses and inabilities of My children. Because of this, I am looking for you to come to the end of yourself and your capabilities, recognizing your need for Me in even the smallest of things. Then, I can work. But you must first step humbly aside, making room for Me. This is not the way of the world around you. It preaches the gospel of self-sufficiency, with its greatest point of pride being to accomplish things apart from Me. But My children know that apart from Me they can do nothing of any eternal value.

Come to the end of yourself, My precious child. I am ready to carry the load. I require only a humble heart that allows Me to work and then follows Me into it.

JANUARY 10

Why are you troubled, and why do
doubts arise in your hearts?

Luke 24:38

❧

I came to bring peace. Where I am, there is peace. The world is not a peaceful place. It is full of striving mixed with anger, hate, greed, and rebellion. Yet, I call you to live in this world and reach it with My love. *How is this possible?*

Abide in Me as I abide in you. Let Me prepare a luxurious feast table in the very midst of your enemies. Hide beneath the shadow of My wings. Climb up into My strong tower. Even in the midst of great storms, you are only one word away...*Jesus.* I will come to you and hold you close. I will give you My eternal perspective of the trouble before you. We will share My peace while the whirlwind of doubt and fear swirls all around.

Give your doubts and troubles to Me. I long to carry them for you. In the moment of your distress, cry out to Me, and I will come to you!

JANUARY 11

When I sent you out with no moneybag or knapsack
or sandals, did you lack anything?

Luke 22:35

❧

My children must learn to trust Me as we walk together.
Each must come to understand that I bring the necessary
provision into place at precisely the right moment. This is
the exciting journey of faith.

Only I know what lies before you along the path we walk.
You may catch small glimpses, but I see the vastness of the
journey as it stretches to the horizon. Because I know what
I will call you to do, I am responsible to equip you for the
tasks ahead. This is why I ask you to concentrate on the
steps at hand each day. I have not yet given you everything
you need for the future. Even today, you are being equipped
for what is to come, and you are being trained to use what I
am supplying for you. It is not My way to give you too much
too soon. It would not be profitable for you.

Walk with Me and pay close attention to all that is
provided. As you continue with Me, you will lack nothing for
the journey. With this knowledge comes faith. Faith is the
basis of all we will do together.

JANUARY 12

How many loaves do you have?

Mark 6:38

❧

The world is proud in its stance against My children and Me. It is sure that such insignificant ones can have no impact against it. But I have another plan. I take the humble and unimportant and make them to stand against the giants.

I find great joy in multiplying whatever you bring to Me to accomplish My plans. Even a little can be made miraculously into an abundance. I did it with the loaves and fishes. I can do it with your willing heart. You will face many overwhelming obstacles in this life, but I have a purpose for each and every one of them. As you give out of your inadequacy, I show Myself strong on your behalf.

What can one as small as you do against the giants of this world? What do you have to offer that can make an impact? Bring to Me whatever you have. I delight in doing much with your little.

January 13

Do you not yet understand?

Mark 8:21

❧

I am always at work. I move to bring great and small things to pass in your life.

Life can sometimes slip into a haze of habit. The mundane can quickly blind you to the supernatural. Even I can become a common thing to you if you are not careful. The happenings in your life are not a casual squandering of time. They are crafted for My purpose in you and in the world. Look around you. *Do you see Me working?* Consider the past twenty-four hours. What have I done for you? With you? In you?

Open your eyes and learn. See what is happening through My perspective. Then you can understand and gain wisdom.

JANUARY 14

Did I not tell you that if you believed
you would see the glory of God?

John 11:40

❧❧

It is not possible for mankind to understand the fullness of
My glory. The human mind cannot conceive of its brilliant
composition. It is so overwhelming that death would come
instantly.

Moses saw some of My glory. So did Peter, James, and
John. But they did not see all of My glory. Likewise, neither
do you. I do, however, allow you to experience its shadows
in the world around you. Consider the fury of a storm, or
the bright hues of color hidden in the plumage of a bird, or
the majesty of an unspoiled forest, or the perfect crystalline
form of a snowflake. Who can look beneath the sea or into
the vastness of space and not know something of My glory?
Then there are My miracles. They are disruptions of the
physical world by the divine. Whether it is the saving of a
sinner, or the healing of the sick, or the raising of the dead,
the power of My glory is on display for those who have eyes
to see it.

As My child, you are a miracle. I will perform great works
through you if you believe it is possible—My glory displayed
through your hands.

JANUARY 15

Where is your faith?

Luke 8:25

৵৽

Faith is powerful. It is the confidence of knowing that the impossible circumstances of the moment are subject to My unlimited power. By such faith, I can do much with a life.

I am a faithful God. I am fully engaged in your concerns. Together, we will cross many seas that are stirred and stormy. Do not be afraid. If I have called you to do something, will I not also make a way for it to be done? This is where many fall away. They are excited to begin the journey with Me, but as soon as the waves and the winds come, they panic and forget I am with them. They no longer want to take the journey with Me. They think within their hearts, *I didn't sign up for this!*

Do not lose heart! I hold you in My hand. Nothing can touch you unless I allow it. If I allow it, it is for your ultimate benefit. Keep this in mind and your eyes on Me. Let your faith be strong! Much will be done!

JANUARY 16

How can you believe, when you receive
glory from one another and do not seek the
glory that comes from the only God?

John 5:44

❧❧

I search the world over, seeking hearts that are truly Mine. These pursue Me, seeking only to please Me in everything.

Look for My approval in your life. Do not seek the approval of man. My approval is My honor bestowed upon you for your actions. It means that what you are doing is beneficial to the plans I have for you. The approval of man is self-serving. It is temporary and it is fickle. Yet, many make this mistake. They seek the admiration of man instead of the affirmation of God. They do not realize that man's endorsement comes only from an earthly perspective. My approval comes from an eternal perspective. *Which do you think is better?*

Walk the solitary path of My approval. This allows you to do the work I have given you and not be swayed from it because of rejection or for the sake of shallow praise. Seek to please Me above all!

January 17

Have you believed because you have seen me?

John 20:29

❧❧

Much of My work is done in the quiet moments of life. Within the faithful service of My children both heaven and earth are moved.

It is easy to grow weary when you walk through difficulties that seem to have no end. You want to see a big flash of lightning dispel the darkness of your trial. Most of the time, this is not My way. Through trials and tribulation, I am testing and proving your faith. I am teaching you to walk by My power when you do not have any of your own. It is here in perseverance that you will see your faith grow and be made strong, not in the instant deliverance you desire.

Walk with Me by faith, not by sight. Develop the endurance of a heart that waits patiently for Me to move. You will grow mighty in Me and have much to share with others.

JANUARY 18

Do you take offense at this?

John 6:61

❧❧

I am love, unconditional and pure. I speak truth to all who will hear it, and I have the authority to do so. Those who do not like who I am or the words I have spoken regularly take offense. Do not think I am speaking only of the world. I speak also of My children.

I ask much of those who follow Me. Many times this goes far beyond anything they have thought to be appropriate for them. Most have settled into believing in a version of Me that is of their own making. They have put boundaries around what they think I will ask of them. They have constructed traditions and religions that are far from Me. When finally confronted with the truth, many cannot accept it. They find the true Me to be offensive.

I long for you to know Me as I am. Put aside your preconceptions and do not box Me in. Seek Me with a pure heart free of bias. I will reveal Myself to you. I am much more than you think I am.

January 19

Do you want to go away as well?

John 6:67

༚

I work in the lives of My children to bring about the plans My Father has for the world. Each of them has a part to play in this unfolding reality.

I have plainly told you there will be times of trial, tribulation, and trouble in this world. I will also ask you to go and do things that are very difficult or unpopular. When these times come to you and those you love, persevere. When you feel the weight of these troubles overwhelming you, come to Me. I will take your load and help you walk through all you face. When we look back upon these times, you will see My purposes clearly and be unwilling to trade them for an equal amount of ease.

The path I have laid before you is not based on ease or popularity. However, it leads to a life of fulfillment and substance. *Will you walk with Me into the difficult things?*

JANUARY 20

And why do you not judge for yourselves what is right?

Luke 12:57

⫷⫸

I am the Prince of Peace. The hallmark of My followers is that they are peaceable people at heart. Even though they must stand for what is right in this fallen world, everything they do should be salted with My love.

How many times have you become indignant when accused by another? How many times have you judged yourself to be right and others wrong? Are not pride and self-righteousness the sources of such actions and attitudes? Instead, remember your own fallibility and seek the common ground in love. Common ground is not compromise. It is focusing on what is most important and leaving the rest to Me. Only in this way can you avoid the condemnation of others for hypocrisy.

Do not go the way of the Pharisees, judging others to be wrong when you are not right. Instead, examine yourself from their perspectives. A humble attitude and a soft answer turn wrath away.

JANUARY 21

Can a blind man lead a blind man?
Will they not both fall into a pit?

Luke 6:39

༺༻

I came to shine My light into the darkness of the world. If My children will allow it, this illumination can reach into the dark recesses of their hearts and help them to see clearly. As they cooperate with Me in this way, each gains the wisdom of My perspective. Only as they faithfully follow Me can they lead others to see My great truths.

Too many of My children run off with only their perspectives. They spread their view of things far and wide. They have not taken the time to learn of My ways or gain My perspective, nor do they want to. They would rather be busy doing what they think is best than to sit at My feet and discover all that I am. In so doing, they lead many from the path of truth to the way of error. Soon, they are wallowing in the miry darkness of the pit they have fallen into.

Allow Me to do My work in your heart. Learn of Me, My truths, and My ways. Then you can shine the light of My love on the path for others to follow.

January 22

Why does this generation seek a sign?

Mark 8:12

‌‌ *

An evil generation seeks after a sign. I have already given the greatest sign of all—My resurrection after three days in the grave.

I am at work around you. In fact, I never stop working on your behalf. You will see this if you open your spiritual eyes. The clearest evidence of My work in you is your changed heart. I have taken it from being continuously at war with Me and made it Mine. I have transformed what was once dead in sin, making it alive in Me. If you think about it, this is the greatest miracle of all. A life lived for Me is a sign for the whole world to see. But the world and many of My children discount this. They want to see something mystical and spectacular. By this very desire, they reveal their unbelief. For as it was in the days when I walked the earth, one sign or wonder will never be enough for them. They will only seek another more spectacular.

Do not get caught up in the rush to see signs and wonders. Instead, live your life fully for Me out of love. I have called you to be the miracle the world can see. Your devotion will be a testimony against all that is evil until the end of time.

JANUARY 23

Is it lawful to heal on the Sabbath, or not?

Luke 14:3

୧ଡ଼ଃ

My love for My children takes no holiday. I am always present for their benefit. I reach beyond man-made traditions and practices, directly to their needs.

I work in many ways in the lives of My children. Often, My methods do not conform to what is considered to be acceptable. Many of My followers have developed inflexible religious habits. They have decided what can and cannot be done, what is appropriate and what is not. I am much bigger than such thoughts. Rules and regulations cannot constrain Me in My work of love.

I am only concerned with your heart. I invest heavily in healing it and molding it to be like Mine. It does not matter the day of the week. I work when I must, and I invite you into My work.

JANUARY 24

Do you think that I have come to give peace on earth?

Luke 12:51

☙❧

I am the lightning rod of controversy. There is no middle ground with Me. One is either with Me or against Me. One either follows Me or follows their own desires.

I did not come to bring peace as the world defines it—a life free from conflict and trouble and risk. I came to divide those who will be Mine from those who will not. This dividing is the source of much conflict and trouble and risk. Though spiritual in nature, this dividing manifests itself in the physical world as hatred for Me and all who belong to Me. Yet, as My child, you can experience My peace in the midst of it all. How is this possible? By inviting Me into your circumstances. When you do, I help you gain My perspective on your situation. I take the burden from you. I surround you with My presence. This is true peace. All of evil's fury cannot take it from you.

I have called you to live in My peace even as the storm rages around you in the world. This requires that you not get caught up in your circumstances, but instead get caught up in Me.

January 25

And will not God give justice to his elect, who cry to him day and night? Will he delay long over them?

Luke 18:7

❧❧

I am the God of true justice. I have a scale in My hand. I weigh the deeds of all who raise their hand against My children.

As My follower, you will not gain justice in this life. Those who do not follow Me will take advantage of you. The systems of the world will stand against you. You will suffer persecution and be accused of intolerance and narrow-mindedness. In the end, though, I will set everything right. Justice will be meted out for every wrong you have suffered. I will judge the world and all of its practices. The people of the world scoff at the idea that there will be a day of reckoning for their actions. They think I have overlooked their evilness. But that day will come, and their arrogance will vanish like snow in the hot sun. True justice will prevail.

You have been chosen and have heeded the call. Be patient in your sufferings. Know that I see each injustice and will require an accounting from those who have taken advantage of you.

JANUARY 26

*Nevertheless, when the Son of Man
comes, will he find faith on earth?*

Luke 18:8

❧❧

Who will remain faithful in their walk with Me? Who will be the steadfast ones? Only those who cry out to Me with the expectation that I will hear and come to their rescue.

It is easy for My children to lose heart in this life and despair of My delayed justice. Many who do, cease walking with Me. Their faithfulness in the battle fails. They stop crying out to Me and are overwhelmed. Do not lose heart! Though the waves may foam and the wind may roar, you will not be overcome by the storms if you cry out in faith. Keep moving in the direction I have pointed you. Steadily place one foot in front of the other. Hold tight to My hand and gain the advantage of My strength.

Remain steadfast in Me. Walk in faithfulness. When troubles come, do not be quiet. Call, and I will answer. Reach out to My hand, and I will lift you up.

JANUARY 27

Children, do you have any fish?

John 21:5

୭ৠৰ

The ways of mankind are limited. My way is limitless. The wise cease their self-sufficient ways and begin walking in My strength. The foolish wander alone along paths of their own choosing.

It is My great pleasure to help you each day. I wait patiently for you to come to the end of yourself so you are ready for My help. I watch as you toil in your own strength and do what you think is right. At the end of it all, you will have accomplished nothing of value for My kingdom because you have walked the path alone. Many of My children do not recognize the futility of their independent ways. Though they seem to accomplish much in their own eyes and in the eyes of others, their efforts remain a work of the flesh and lack My supernatural power.

Cease your fruitless laboring. Stop and invite Me into the effort. I will give you direction and add My power to your weakness. Together, we can accomplish what needs to be done, leaving the wasted efforts behind.

JANUARY 28

Why do you call me 'Lord, Lord,' and not do what I tell you?

Luke 6:46

❧

The marks of My true disciples are their love for Me and their willingness to go where I lead them. They hear My voice calling to them, and they respond in obedience.

Many of My children profess love for Me but do not follow Me. For these uncommitted ones, shallow emotions have replaced obedience. They are double-minded, trying to serve two masters—their own foolish desires and Me. I cannot rely on them to accomplish anything of heavenly value. Others have deceived themselves. They say that they belong to Me, but they do not. I do not live in their hearts. This is why they do not follow Me or do what I ask.

I am your Lord. I call out to you each day. I invite you to follow Me and do the things I ask of you. I long to teach you My ways and make you My disciple. *Will you follow Me?*

January 29

Do you understand what I have done to you?

John 13:12

❧

I am your Teacher and your Lord. Yet, I bowed low to lift you up. I became a servant to demonstrate My love for you.

I died so you could live. I suffered persecution as God in the flesh so you could bear it also as My disciples. I sacrificed My life day after day to show you the way. I opened the gate to let you into an eternity with Me. I defeated death to remove its sting from this earthly life. I marched over Satan so you could walk in victory. I lived a sinless life to encourage you to do the same. I knew pain, hunger, thirst, and weariness so you could count on My understanding. In all this and more, I served you so you could learn to serve others.

My beloved, live life to the fullest in Me. I have made a way for you. Follow Me, serving others in love and with mercy.

JANUARY 30

Simon, son of John, do you love me more than these?

John 21:15

ॐ

I love you. You are My special creation. My Father called you before the foundations of the world were ever laid. My love is not fickle. It does not ebb and flow with what you do or how you perform. It is unconditional, and it is unfailing.

It is easy to get caught up in the things of this life—the people, the possessions, the positions, and the noise. These can carry away your affections. They can become your idols, replacing Me, the rightful object of your love and devotion. Many of My children have allowed their affections to turn from Me, their first love. These have been swept away by the things of the world. Yet, if asked, they would profess their love for Me. These do not comprehend how far from Me they are and how close to the world they have become. *Am I merely an acquaintance to you?*

Learn to love Me as I love you. Delight in My presence as I delight in yours. Invest your heart in Mine. We have an eternity to spend together, and it has already begun.

January 31

Will you lay down your life for me?

John 13:38

❧

Many have made it a practice to generalize the answer to this question. They have convinced themselves that by proclaiming to belong to Me, they have already laid down their lives. I tell you plainly, these have deceived themselves.

The salvation moment is only the first step of a life laid at My feet. Becoming My disciple is the daily process of dying to self and living for Me. Only by doing this are you laying your life down as I have asked. Laying down one's life is an act of the will. It is a choice that is made moment by moment each day. Every act reveals its reason. Every decision reveals the heart. *What are you laying your life down for?*

I know that dying to yourself is repulsive to your flesh. The flesh wants to cling to life and have its way. I ask for your full devotion to Me. Take My hand. I will help you die each day. You will then discover that you are truly beginning to live.

FEBRUARY

Jesus taught of the powerful relationship between prayer, faith, and His will. With these three in alignment, a humble petition before a mighty God has the power to move mountains.

FEBRUARY 1

And I tell you, ask, and it will be given to you; seek, and
you will find; knock, and it will be opened to you.

Luke 11:9

⌘

How have you prayed to Me? Was it a quiet word or a long
searching conversation of many days? Did you desperately
pound on the throne room door?

Prayer is action. Your petition is given life by words
spoken from a humble heart. It can be as simple as asking
Me to do something. It can progress on and become a
diligent searching for answers. It can even end up as an
urgent knocking on the very throne room door of heaven.
Regardless of the form, effort must be put into the request.

I hear not only the prayer, but I observe the method used
as well. Each of these—asking, seeking, and knocking—is
appropriate depending upon the situation. Each reveals the
determination of your heart.

FEBRUARY 2

If you ask me anything in my name, I will do it.

John 14:14

᎒᎒

I have plans for the lives of each of My children. These are far beyond what they can imagine because they come from the throne of My Father.

Prayer helps you get your heart in line with My plans. You have needs and wants, and you have expectations of when and how these should be satisfied. When you seek Me with an open heart, I work to help you understand if your requests fit into My will for your life and what should be done with those that don't. Many do not understand this. They believe that by simply adding the words *in Jesus' name* at the end of a prayer, I am bound to do for them all they have asked or to put My blessing on their various activities. This is a great deception that leads many astray. Praying in My name is praying in My will—a process that must be *labored through* by way of an honest conversation with Me. It is the great work of asking, seeking, and knocking in alignment with My plans for you.

Examine your prayers to see if we are in step with one another. Let Me change the desires of your heart to be as Mine. This draws us into the close fellowship of a shared purpose.

FEBRUARY 3

*If you had faith like a grain of mustard seed, you
could say to this mulberry tree, 'Be uprooted and
planted in the sea,' and it would obey you.*

Luke 17:6

❧

Prayer connects the natural to the supernatural, the finite
to the infinite, and the thoughts of man to the purposes of
God.

Your prayers must be built on a foundation of faith.
Believe that praying matters. Believe the petition is heard.
Believe that supernatural action will be taken on your
behalf. Many do not pray in faith. Instead, they pray from
habit. Well-worn words tumble from their lips, but the
heart is not engaged. Words alone are not prayers. They
must be rooted in faith deep within the heart. I can take the
feeblest faith behind a request and work extraordinary
miracles.

How do you pray? Is there a grain of faith that believes I
will hear and can do all you have asked? Or do you speak
words of emptiness? Give Me at least a mustard seed of
faith. I await to do marvelous things for you and through
you!

FEBRUARY 4

For everyone who asks receives, and the one who seeks finds, and to the one who knocks it will be opened.

Luke 11:10

୭⳿ᦲ

It is My great delight to answer the prayers of My children. After they have spoken to Me, I begin to work.

When you pray, I may answer quickly, or I may be silent. I may affirm your request, or I may help you to understand it is not in line with My will. You may see mountains begin to move slowly in the foggy distance or instant miracles performed in your midst. You may even see things happening that seem to have nothing to do with your request. But I will work so My plans for you can come to pass. Many discount prayer in this busy world. Some reason that there is no purpose for prayer because the petition is already known by an omniscient God. Others have decided that praying is useless because a sovereign God cannot be moved by such requests. These do not know the power of a heart-to-heart conversation with Me.

When you ask in My name with faith, answers are received, things searched for are found, and doors are opened in the midst of impossible situations. Such prayers draw you into My presence and make My perfect will known to you. At this place of submission, My power is released in your life.

FEBRUARY 5

*If you then, who are evil, know how to give good gifts
to your children, how much more will the heavenly
Father give the Holy Spirit to those who ask him!*

Luke 11:13

પ્જ્જ

Every good gift comes down from My Father. It is My
pleasure to pass all that is in His will to My children.

You can depend on My faithfulness toward you. I am not
a capricious God who toys with your emotions and needs. I
seek to equip you for all I have planned for you. It is My
great desire that we would be one in spirit in the same
manner as My Father and I are. I do not want you to
struggle needlessly through life, trying this or that in an
effort to survive. I want you to *thrive!*

For this reason, you have been given the Holy Spirit. He
lives within you and can guide you to know Me better. Ask
for His help in knowing Me. The more you know Me, the
more you understand My will. This makes your prayers
effective and powerful.

FEBRUARY 6

He [Holy Spirit] will glorify me, for he will
take what is mine and declare it to you.

John 16:14

૭๛๛

Each of My children *can* learn to pray effectively in My
name. The Holy Spirit will teach them how.

The Holy Spirit dwells in each of My children. It is He
who helps you know My heart so you can pray in My will.
His main purpose is to glorify Me and make Me known to
you. The more you know Me, the more you will understand
My heart for you and the faster you can get your heart in
line with Mine. My heart always reflects My will. There can
be times when you do not know what to pray for, times
when you are so burdened that you cannot even speak. I
assure you, the Holy Spirit knows what to pray on your
behalf, and He will petition the throne of God for you. His
prayers are aligned with My will for you, so they are
powerful. As a result of His work, your understanding of My
will increases, bringing us into harmony.

I long to be in step with you! Together, we can overcome
any obstacle you encounter in life. And we can do it
effectively according to My plans for you. Take heart at this
great truth!

FEBRUARY 7

Therefore I tell you, whatever you ask in prayer,
believe that you have received it, and it will be yours.

Mark 11:24

ॐॐ

Prayer removes burdens. It causes them to be laid down at
My feet.

When you pray, you transfer a burden from your life to
Me. It is a great pleasure for Me to accept the burden from
you and carry it. You know when the handoff occurs
because you feel a sense of release in your soul. My peace
invades your storm, confirming that you have given the
burden to Me. Once you have done this, believe that I am
taking care of your situation in My way and My timing.
Trust that I am at work somehow and in some way. This is
walking in faith. It is here, though, that many fall. They
come to Me as beggars with hearts full of wishful thinking.
They are only hopeful but do not truly believe.

Remember you are My child whom I love. Come
confidently to Me. Lay your petition at My feet. Leave
trusting by faith that I will do what is in line with My will,
which is always what is best for you.

FEBRUARY 8

Whatever you ask in my name, this I will do,
that the Father may be glorified in the Son.

John 14:13

༄ঌ

I always seek to bring glory and honor to My Father. I do this by executing His plans for this age in both the spiritual and physical realms. Each of My children has a part in this.

As My child, you have special access to the details of My Father's plans. When you pray in My name, you are actually seeking to gain greater access and participation in these plans. Understand this clearly! It is a great honor bestowed by Him upon all who love and offer service to Me. Those who pray in their own wills and after their own desires miss this great opportunity. They cannot see beyond what they want to what My Father desires.

My son or daughter, there is no higher calling than to be allowed to join in the plans of God. As you enter into these plans through prayer, our Father is glorified.

FEBRUARY 9

*Pray then like this: Our Father in
heaven, hallowed be your name.*

Matthew 6:9

❧

Effective prayer comes from a humble heart. Humbleness is understanding one's true state before a holy God.

It is true you are a child of God if you belong to Me. You have been adopted into My family and share an eternity together with all who belong to Me. The humble always realize the source of these great privileges. They understand fully their truthful reality apart from My power working in their lives. Many, however, do not consider this when they come to pray. They fail to acknowledge their spiritual bankruptcy apart from Me. Instead, they come boldly before the very throne of a holy God with their demands. Such presumption lacks the underlying humbleness I seek in My children who come to pray.

Come before the throne of grace unafraid, but come humbly. Acknowledge the One who sits on the throne and His holiness. Remember that My blood has covered your sin, making your approach possible. A heart in such a state is a heart that can both hear and be heard.

FEBRUARY 10

*Your kingdom come, your will be
done, on earth as it is in heaven.*

Matthew 6:10

❧

Rejoice that the kingdom of God is at hand! Rejoice that it lives in your heart! Rejoice that you are a part of bringing it to fruition upon the earth in the hearts of others!

Many mumble these very words without understanding what they mean. Even so, these words have great weight as they spill forth from the lips of those who utter them. They are a declaration that the plans of God should be the plans of those who are praying. Many are condemned by these words because this is not the intent of their hearts. They do not want My Father's will for their lives, only their own.

My child, when you pray, do so from a heart that is fully aligned to what I am doing in the world around you and in your own heart. Be found faithful in this. The kingdom of God is at hand.

FEBRUARY 11

Give us this day our daily bread.

Matthew 6:11

Little children, I am your provider. All that is good in your life comes through Me. *Think on this.*

Most of My children pay only lip service to My providing their daily bread. They have vague notions that I take care of them, but they think differently in their hearts. They truly believe that they provide for themselves. Even worse, they think it is their responsibility to do so. I ask you to believe it is My responsibility to provide for you. Then be ready to accept the way I choose to do this. It may be quite different from how you would go about it. I provide based on what I am working to accomplish in your life. You provide based on what you are trying to achieve. Which would you say is the more excellent way? Which would you say puts you on My path?

If you allow it, I will show you what I want you to do for a job, a career, or a vocation. When you obey Me in this, I am responsible for supplying your needs. I carry the burden for your daily bread, not you. If, however, you go off on your own, you are responsible to support yourself. I stand aside and allow you to do so. *How will you obtain your daily bread?*

FEBRUARY 12

*And forgive us our debts, as we
also have forgiven our debtors.*

Matthew 6:12

❧

Forgiveness is a part of rightly judging others. You will be
wronged by many in your lifetime, both from the world and
from My Church. Your responsibility is to forgive others as I
have forgiven you. I no longer look upon your sins, nor do I
look upon who you once were. I see only My righteousness
and the person I created you to be.

Many hold their hurts and slights tightly to themselves.
They harshly judge their perpetrators for the wrongs these
have committed. They do not understand that by doing this
they enslave themselves in hate and drink the poison of
bitterness. They do not see that their sin of unforgiveness
keeps them in bondage and opens doors for demonic
activity.

Do not hinder your prayers by withholding forgiveness
from others. Grant it while it is yet *today.* Remain free from
the bondage of this sin. Look upon others from My
perspective. See them as I see them. When you pray, come
to Me humbly in awe of My continuing forgiveness of the
displeasing things you do each day.

FEBRUARY 13

And lead us not into temptation, but deliver us from evil.

Matthew 6:13

⌘

Evil is a reality that each of My children must face. It is ever present along the path we travel.

The evil ones lie in wait for you each day. They know your past failings and how to attack you. The bigger the plans I have for you, the more intently they seek My permission to sift you like wheat and expose your chaff. They then accuse you more vehemently before Me, arguing for greater access to your life. I am your protector and your deliverer. My grace allows you to walk fearlessly in the midst of evil. My mercy limits the extent to which the demonic world can seek to tempt and trap you.

Ask Me each day to work in your heart so your weaknesses can be made strong. Ask Me to keep you from the baseness of your flesh. Ask Me to deny the request of more evil access to your soul. Ask Me to keep you from turning to the left or the right off of the path I have chosen for you. Then, walk according to the high calling with which I have called you.

February 14

*Truly, truly, I say to you, whatever you ask of
the Father in my name, he will give it to you.*

John 16:23

❧❧

A prayer spoken in My name according to My will reaches
the very throne room of heaven. It rises as the smoke of
incense, a sweet-smelling cry from a pure heart.

My Father who sits enthroned in thunder and lightning
and every color of the rainbow hears such prayers, as do I.
Because He has given all authority to Me, I am free to act
upon your petitions according to My will, which is also His.
Some make it a habit of praying amiss to My Father. They
speak from a need or want that is not in line with His
plans. I tell you, these prayers are not heard by Him nor do
they come before His throne.

My children, you have a God in heaven who savors the
aroma of prayers from a humble heart. Pray aright so His
will may be done on earth for you as it is done in heaven.

FEBRUARY 15

*Again I say to you, if two of you agree on earth
about anything they ask, it will be done for them by
my Father in heaven. For where two or three are
gathered in my name, there am I among them.*

Matthew 18:19-20

❦

I am attentive to the cries of My children. There is a special urgency when they gather together to pray with one heart.

Much power comes from hearts that are intertwined and focused on a common request. During these times, I come so close that I become another cord in the rope of this agreement, lending it My strength. The opposite is also true. Even though an entire building of people lift their hearts as one in a prayer, if that prayer is amiss, I will not come close. Many have been deceived in this way, thinking a corporate prayer is valid because it was sanctioned by a religious figure. I tell you, whoever leads such a prayer will be held accountable for its content. Be mindful of your prayers!

Join with others in seeking My face. The power of a simple petition is multiplied exponentially when shared with others because I am in your midst.

FEBRUARY 16

And when you pray, you must not be like the hypocrites.
For they love to stand and pray in the synagogues and at
the street corners, that they may be seen by others. Truly,
I say to you, they have received their reward.

Matthew 6:5

৵৵

I love to hear My children talk to Me. This is the essence of prayer—a conversation between man and God. *Think on this, and stand in amazement.*

There are those who love to pray in public. They seek the adoration of others for their eloquent words and their pious posture. Their hearts are far from Me. They only seek the attention of those around them. I am not impressed with their spiritual boasting. They have all they will receive as a reward for their prayers in the fleeting admiration of their audience.

Do not be like these. Do not seek the praise of others. Seek Me and My approval. Your reward will be great.

FEBRUARY 17

But when you pray, go into your room and shut the
door and pray to your Father who is in secret. And
your Father who sees in secret will reward you.

Matthew 6:6

Prayer is an intimate meeting between man and God. It is a conversation between the mortal and the divine. During prayer, the hearts of My children are opened to the heart of God.

I listen intently for words spoken to Me from a humble heart. When we talk together in this way, it is a sweet time of closeness. Though the words we speak are between us, their benefit reaches out to many. It is in these quiet moments that you are made strong. My peace settles upon you, and you float in its gentle warmth. Time stands still in the quietness. The noise of the world is blotted out. All that matters is that we are together.

Seek Me in the quiet places. I will meet you there. Find Me throughout the day. I take great joy in talking to you!

FEBRUARY 18

And when you pray, do not heap up empty
phrases as the Gentiles do, for they think that
they will be heard for their many words.

Matthew 6:7

❧

Prayer is talking to Me and waiting for Me to answer. It is
not enhanced by a multitude of words.

The words you speak reflect your heart, the object of My
concern. As we talk together, your heart becomes aligned
with Mine. Soon, you come to know My will so we can be in
agreement. Do not recite prayers from memory or use
learned church-speak! Do not pile high-sounding phrases
one upon another in an effort to give your prayer a measure
of religious credibility. Instead, talk to Me as a friend talks
to another—with intense sincerity from the heart.

Pray with purpose. Speak to Me from the recesses of
your heart. I will respond with the same sincerity. Our
conversation will be of great consequence in your life.

FEBRUARY 19

*Do not be like them, for your Father knows
what you need before you ask him.*

Matthew 6:8

❧

I hold the entire universe together, atom by atom. A
sparrow cannot fall from the sky without My notice, nor can
a loose hair fall from your head. I am in the details of your
life because you are My beloved. *Stop and consider this.*

Many pray from their wants. They recite long lists filled
with the desires of their hearts. These can be sincere
prayers offered with intense longing, and many times, the
things being sought are not bad or wrong. However, they
are one-sided conversations with little consideration given
to what I have to say in response. Often, it is not the time
or the place for Me to grant the wants, and those who have
prayed become angry, discouraged, or disillusioned.

I have a better way for you. I know *exactly* what you need
and I know *precisely* when you need it. These needs are
necessary for you to become all I intend and perfectly timed
for you to accomplish all I have planned. Gain this
perspective when you pray. Ask for what you need, and
then allow for My timing. I will add many of your wants
along the way.

FEBRUARY 20

The Pharisee, standing by himself, prayed thus: 'God,
I thank you that I am not like other men, extortioners,
unjust, adulterers, or even like this tax collector.'

Luke 18:11

❧

The proud speak from their self-righteousness. Their words
come from their elevated opinion of themselves and their
low opinion of others.

I love you for who you are becoming—that vision of you I
had in mind before I formed you in your mother's womb. I
know you are a work in progress. I have not yet lifted you
from My pottery wheel. I do not compare or contrast you
with other vessels I have made for My service. I judge you
on your own. There are those who do not share this
perspective. Their self-worth is not measured by what I see
in them. Instead, it is a product of comparing themselves
with others. This is the basis for self-righteousness, and the
root of it is pride. It is the source of endless hypocrisy
among My people.

Others are not the measuring rods of your worth to Me.
You are priceless! Remember that you are a work in
progress, and thank Me from a grateful heart.

FEBRUARY 21

*But the tax collector, standing far off, would not
even lift up his eyes to heaven, but beat his breast,
saying, 'God, be merciful to me, a sinner!'*

Luke 18:13

☙❧

The deadliest sin of all is pride. It caused Satan to rebel,
and many have been taken captive by it since. There is only
one antidote for pride—a humble heart.

A humble heart is aware of its limits. It knows that only
My supernatural work has given it worth. It realizes that
apart from Me, nothing good can come of it. It seeks My
power to do its work. It harbors all the fruits of the Holy
Spirit and cherishes them. It loves what I love and hates
what I hate. It puts itself last and esteems others as
greater. It stands before Me in awe. It seeks to become more
like Me.

I can do much with your humble heart. It is the
springboard of all My work in you. Out of it, I can flow to
everyone you touch. By this, the world is blessed through
you.

FEBRUARY 22

'If you can'! All things are possible for one who believes.

Mark 9:23

❧

Evidence of My majesty is found throughout all of creation. My power is alive and can be found in My faithful disciples. Take a look around you. *Can you see it?*

Even so, there are many of My children who doubt I will move the mountains in their lives. They come to Me almost apologetically with their requests. What they seek seems so fantastic to them that they are afraid it is too much to ask of Me. They are held captive by the very miracle they seek, unable to move forward without it and afraid to believe it can be done.

I am an able God. I stretch out My hand for you to grasp. Talk to Me about the mountain that blocks your path. Let us reason together about the miracle of moving it out of your way. Regardless of its lofty height or great mass, believe in My ability to cast it aside.

FEBRUARY 23

O you of little faith, why did you doubt?

Matthew 14:31

৵৽

I have called you to walk with Me upon the water. Yes, to you it seems an impossible request that is too much for Me to ask of you. Nevertheless, I am asking. *What will you do?*

My children spend too much of their time seeing all that is impossible in their walk with Me. Day after day, I call them to move beyond their comfort zones and step out of their boats and onto the water. But they look at the wind and waves as they grip the sources of their security ever more tightly and will not move. Their refusal to take the first step into the impossible dooms them to an ineffective and powerless life.

I am calling out to you. It is time to leave the boat. Do not find your security in the things of this world. Instead, believe that My outstretched hand is the only true security. Walk on the water with Me. We will find a path between the waves.

FEBRUARY 24

Do not fear; only believe...

Luke 8:50

৵৽

What man or woman thinks they know the path they will walk in this life? Only the foolish who have deceived themselves.

You cannot see into the future. You may think you can, but you cannot. The path fades before you into the haze of uncertainty. Even what you will be doing tomorrow is in doubt if you are wise. This keeps you dependent on Me. As I guide you down the path I have chosen for your life, I tell you the next step to take. There will be times when I ask you to step into the dark where you cannot see. Do not give heed to the voices around you who warn of the foolishness of taking this step. You will be justified in your faithful obedience to Me as your foot lands solidly on My path.

I have invested much in you. I have shown you the narrow path we walk. I am equipping you for what is coming next. *Will you take My hand in faith and walk with Me?*

FEBRUARY 25

Go your way; your faith has made you well.

Mark 10:52

࿇

Your faith is essential to walk where I am leading you. It is what sustains you when the way takes a turn you did not expect.

Many of My children stumble over the circumstances in their lives. They think linearly, ordering their expectations in a way that seems right to them. They cannot see how it is possible to go from point A to point C unless we first pass through point B. Their faith is not enough for them to believe beyond what their minds can conceive. They remain in blindness, and their walk is hindered. I have called you to your own unique journey with Me. I cannot tell you the details of the full journey because your heart could not bear them. Instead, I reveal each day step by step. This way, you only need enough faith to get through today.

Even if the path we walk does not make sense to you, have enough faith for this day. Soon, you will see clearly why we are walking where we are.

FEBRUARY 26

For this statement [of faith] you may go your
way; the demon has left your daughter.

Mark 7:29

৵৽

Your faith is essential to the walk of others. What you ask of Me on their behalf can greatly affect their lives—just like the mother asking on behalf of her daughter.

Even though you are on your own unique journey, I cause your path to intersect the paths of others. For a time, you walk together with them, and then you branch off once again. I do this for a purpose—that your testimony and faith may help others in their individual walks with Me. Many of My children run in herds. They like to stay with the pack and do what they have always done. These resist My leading to branch out and touch other lives. They miss opportunities to grow their faith and the faith of others.

My way for you is not the way of the herd. For the sake of all My children, I give you different opportunities to experience Me. You can then encourage others to follow Me into places you and I have already traversed. In this way, your individuality brings a blessing to them.

FEBRUARY 27

Take heart, daughter; your faith has made you well.

Matthew 9:22

❦

Faith changes things. It keeps you involved with what I am doing. It unleashes My power in your circumstances. In this way, faith is essential for you to do what I am asking of you.

Each of My children encounters obstacles in their path. There is no walk with Me void of challenges. Some are small and can be stepped over with little effort. Others are monumental, blocking all advances. This is where many become stymied. The way that was once easy becomes insurmountable. They cannot go forward, though they try. They fall back in defeat. Some even give up, blaming Me for not making the way easier. These forget to ask, seek, and knock in faith. I stand ready to assist, but they are not up to the effort required.

I do not want this to happen to you! Talk to Me as we walk along the way. Bring Me into your challenges. Cling to Me and do not let go until I infuse your life with My power so the obstacles can be overcome.

FEBRUARY 28

Is it not written, 'My house shall be called a house of prayer for all the nations'? But you have made it a den of robbers.

Mark 11:17

❧

It is time to clean your house. Clutter is piled high. Neglect has made it a shambles. It is no longer agile but has become sodden and lost its vibrancy. I speak of your life and your home. *Sit quietly before Me. Can you see what I mean?*

The same has happened within My Church. On the one hand, bureaucracy and conformity have nearly strangled the life from it. On the other, it has drowned in the new wine of errant spiritual experiences and lost all sense of itself. Neither of these is My way. What does either offer to the world? A dead religion based on a dead man? Or, perhaps, a shallow religion based on error, emotions, and covetousness? I have rejected both.

Wake up, My child! I want you to stay in step with Me as I move. Do not be weighed down with the things of the world. Do not allow its entanglements to slow your progress. We have much to do.

FEBRUARY 29

Have faith in God.

Mark 11:22

᷇᷇᷇

You will see Me do many things throughout your life. You will easily accept some, and you will struggle to understand others. Always look with spiritual eyes so you can see My hand moving and doing all around you. This will make your faith strong.

Many reject Me as I am. They attempt to limit Me by defining Me on their terms. Even while seeing what I am doing, they refuse to believe. They lash out at those who truly love Me and have given their lives for My use. These I pity. They have chosen to remain shackled by their religion instead of following freely where I lead.

Grow your faith. Go on the offensive with Me, leaving the safety of conformity behind. I am so much more than most have allowed Me to be.

MARCH

Jesus showed us a new kingdom and invited us to join Him in it. The kingdom of heaven exists upon the earth in the hearts of all who belong to Him. It is unstoppable. It is full of love and life.

MARCH 1

My kingdom is not of this world.

John 18:36

❧❧

I am the King of all kings and the Lord of all lords. Mine is a kingdom of yielded hearts. It lives and moves beyond any structure or program man can devise.

If you look with spiritual eyes, you will see that My kingdom is different from what many are trying to build in this world. These have decided what My kingdom *must* look like. They construct for themselves large edifices in My name. They strive to conscript the peoples of the earth and place them under their version of My banner. Organizations are built, and men sit at the top on their thrones. This is not My way. My kingdom knows no denominational bounds. It is not constrained by what the mind of man can conceive. It is not contained in buildings or maintained on campuses. Only I sit at the top on its throne.

Do not be defined by religious structures or programs. You are a true manifestation of My kingdom in the world. Allow Me to shine forth as the Ruler of your heart so all who see will know My kingdom is not of this world.

MARCH 2

*The time is fulfilled, and the kingdom of God is
at hand; repent and believe in the gospel.*

Mark 1:15

❧❧

My kingdom is here. Its purpose is significant. Those who
are a part of it have specific assignments from Me.

Too many of My children walk through life without a
sense of destiny. They do not see their role in the fulfillment
of My Father's plans for this age. Though a part of My
kingdom, they fail to grasp the significance of this reality.
They wander about as if in a fog. But I have placed you in
the world at this precise time. I have located you perfectly
for all you are to do. My plan for you is in place. There has
been no mistake. Seek it and grasp hold of it!

I say to you, turn from your sluggishness! Understand
the power of My message lived out faithfully in your life! My
kingdom is here. Find your place in it. Ask Me, and I will
show you where.

MARCH 3

The kingdom of God is not coming
in ways that can be observed...

Luke 17:20

❧

I am daily building My kingdom. I do it in ways that will astound you.

My kingdom is not like a tempest. It does not sound like the roar of waves. Thunder does not signal its approach. Though man would make an urgent plea, he cannot will it to appear. It is not found in the multitude of words. Pompous proclamations will not make it so. Rules and regulations cannot bring it forth. It has no place in force or compromise. Instead, it quietly grows as the Holy Spirit works in the hearts of mankind.

Look into your heart. What do you see? It is in this secret place that My kingdom grows. Day upon day My power transforms you from the inside out. Allow Me to do My work in you.

MARCH 4

*...nor will they say, 'Look, here it is!' or 'There!' for
behold, the kingdom of God is in the midst of you.*

Luke 17:21

❧☙

All power in heaven and on earth has been given to Me. Yet,
I have chosen to work one heart at a time in the world. By
this, My kingdom is built.

My children often forget this is My way. They point to
their programs. They praise their personalities. They count
their numbers. Some claim to have proven methods. Others
say they have a special anointing. Each points to *their* way
as *the* way of the kingdom. In all of their scheming, they
look in the wrong direction for success. They rely on their
efforts instead of looking to Me, the One who is building the
kingdom by the power of the Holy Spirit.

I am building My kingdom. Heart upon heart, I add to it
each day. Your heart is My greatest work. I am moving it
from darkness and illuminating it with My love. I am
removing its stony hardness and making it beat in time
with My own.

MARCH 5

You are not far from the kingdom of God.

Mark 12:34

❧

The Holy Spirit draws each person toward the kingdom. He works to make Me known in their heart. Understanding leads to more understanding. Soon, all is clear. All that remains is to walk through the door and enter in.

My kingdom is conspicuous because of its spiritual nature. It is not based on the efforts of man, nor does it depend upon his intellectual reasoning. Even emotions find no place in it. The Holy Spirit moves on the heart. He makes understanding blossom out of knowledge. The heart responds to Him.

Give the Holy Spirit free reign in your heart. Allow Him to do My great work in you. He works from My great love for you. For such is the kingdom of God.

MARCH 6

Children, how difficult it is to enter the kingdom of God!

Mark 10:24

৯১৯

There is only one way into the kingdom. The door is too narrow for the many ways of man.

My Father gave Me the keys to the kingdom. I have unlocked the door for you by My blood shed on your behalf. I have broken the power of sin and death, making a way for you. I have given simple directions for you to find the way of eternal life. All of this was done because of My great love for you. The majority of people who hear this truth reject it. They will not accept the way I have made because they will not accept Me. They think in their hearts they have a better way, one more acceptable to them. They condemn themselves because of their pride. They cannot enter into My kingdom on their terms.

In My love for you, I woo you through the Holy Spirit. I make My way known to you. I invite you to enter into My kingdom. I ask you to follow Me, dying to yourself and living an eternity with Me.

MARCH 7

Truly, I say to you, whoever does not receive the
kingdom of God like a child shall not enter it.

Mark 10:15

 প্রত্তি

My kingdom belongs to those who have hearts like a child.
Such faith opens the door to them.

To follow Me is to love Me with a childlike faith. This faith
is trusting and innocent. It receives what it is given with
wonder and great joy. It longs to be close to Me, the object
of its affection. This type of faith gains entrance into My
kingdom. Pride cannot force its way into My kingdom. Many
have tried and failed. With their minds they have schemed
to find a way, but their hearts are not open to receive the
truth. Pride causes its keeper to stumble and fall. It cools
the heart and keeps it far from Me.

My way is the way of a child. It is the way of a humble
heart. It is the way of salvation. It is the way of kingdom
living. My way calls out to you. *Will you answer like a child?*

MARCH 8

Let the children come to me; do not hinder
them, for to such belongs the kingdom of God.

Mark 10:14

❧❧

My children live by faith. They trust Me fully. They go where
I lead. They allow Me to do My great work through them.
They do not question My methods. They seek to do what I
ask of them above all things because of their great love for
Me.

Many reject such faith. They cannot see how I could
work in such a simplistic way. To them, it is foolishness.
These often persecute others who live by this type of faith,
making them outcasts. They do this because such faith
disrupts their perfectly ordered religious worlds. It shakes
all they have built by their own efforts. It challenges their
version of who I am and how I operate. Deep down, they are
convicted by the purity of trust and the simplicity such
faith makes of this life.

I desire for you to live by this type of faith. I long for you
to trust Me this deeply. I can do much through you when
you live this way. It is a great testimony to others about the
power of My kingdom living in you.

MARCH 9

*Truly, I say to you, only with difficulty will a
rich person enter the kingdom of heaven.*

Matthew 19:23

≈≪

Many come to the door of My kingdom carrying the things
of the world. They seek entrance based upon what they
have. These are denied access because of what they do not
have—Me.

My kingdom is not of this world. It is spiritual. It is Me
pursuing your heart, transforming you into My likeness by
the power of the Holy Spirit. It is you allowing Me to work
through your changed life to touch the lives of others.
People full of the world have a difficult time entering My
kingdom. Many of them want Me *plus* their current
lifestyles and life choices. They do not want to lay their lives
completely down at My feet, which is a requirement for
salvation.

I want all of you. This is what I paid for on the cross of
your salvation. I can do much when I have your heart. You
don't have to be perfect, just willing.

MARCH 10

*Again I tell you, it is easier for a camel to go
through the eye of a needle than for a rich
person to enter the kingdom of God.*

Matthew 19:24

༔

I am truly the God of miracles. Each of My children is a
miracle in their own right. Each has a story about their life
before I intervened and how it changed after I came alive in
them. *What is your story?*

Many in My Church try to make salvation easy for
others. I understand this tendency of the human heart, but
salvation is not easy. The more a person has—indeed, the
more things they rely on in this life apart from Me—the
more difficult it is for them to enter My kingdom.
Possessions, positions, and power cannot force their way
into My kingdom. All must be laid at My feet. Camels are
large. Needles are small.

Salvation is based on faith. It is trusting Me not only
with your eternity but with this life as well. Allow Me to
begin taking care of you. Trust that I know what is best.

MARCH 11

But many who are first will be last, and the last first.

Mark 10:31

❧

I search the world over for the humble heart. I seek those who will draw near to Me, those willing to forsake all to go where I send them and do what I ask of them. The weak I make strong. The prideful I bring to nothing.

The world runs counter to My kingdom. Its sense of privilege, rights, and might have no place in My kingdom. Those who push to the front are not those who remain standing there in the end. Those who covet importance now will discover what is truly important later. At the feast table in My kingdom, the servant is seated in the place of honor, and the prideful one sits far from Me. Hear what I am saying! *What is your profit if you are first during this short life and last for all of eternity in My kingdom?*

My child, when you humble yourself and serve those I have given you to serve, you bring glory to Me, and My light shines out into the dark world. When you stoop low to do as I ask, you stand tall in the kingdom of heaven.

MARCH 12

Truly, I say to you, among those born of women there has arisen no one greater than John the Baptist. Yet the one who is least in the kingdom of heaven is greater than he.

Matthew 11:11

❧❧

As My child, you have great value! You are indeed My pride and joy. I speak fondly of you to My Father. You bring glory to Me, and this brings glory to Him. Your acts of obedience and your sufferings on My behalf are jewels in your eternal crown.

I have many devoted prophets and heroes of the faith from the past. The lists of their exploits with Me are found throughout the pages of Scripture. Yet, each of these could not clearly see the wondrous fulfillment of their faith during their lifetime. They could not see the kingdom as it came into being through Me. But you have. It is a great privilege to be counted among those who have seen the culmination of My promise.

You are a part of the unfolding kingdom of God. Keep this from becoming common to you. Never lose its wonder. Grasp hold of it fully. Let us walk into it in all of its glory.

MARCH 13

From the days of John the Baptist until now the kingdom of heaven has suffered violence, and the violent take it by force.

Matthew 11:12

❧

My kingdom is exploding into being all around you. It is happening in amazing places and in astonishing ways. It is not possible to hold it back. Its force is overwhelming.

Some of My children have lost their sense of urgency about the kingdom of God. Once in, they take their rest or wander aimlessly about without direction. They float through life by habit and rote. They do not press forward, following Me fully into this new life. They have forgotten I have plans great and small for them. Others, though, clearly see what is happening. These rush to the kingdom like an army taking a walled city. They find the way in. They live their new life to the fullest each day. They carry the kingdom with them as they walk in the world.

My child, remember the excitement you felt when you first entered through the gate of My kingdom. Recall your commitment to follow Me into the ranks of My great army on earth. Never lose the urgency of our walk together. Live it with great anticipation!

MARCH 14

*The kingdom of heaven is like a grain of mustard seed
that a man took and sowed in his field. It is the smallest
of all seeds, but when it has grown it is larger than all the
garden plants and becomes a tree, so that the birds of the
air come and make nests in its branches.*

Matthew 13:31-32

৵৶

The world stands in amazement at how something so
significant has grown from something so humble. Much
effort has been made to pluck it from the earth, but its root
remains strong.

My kingdom is of the humblest beginnings. Though God,
I took on the flesh of man and walked among the people of
the earth. At first, one believed in the great news of Our
redemptive plan for mankind, then another and another.
Before long, the tender shoot had grown into a mighty tree
upon the earth. Though the forces of evil have besieged this
tree, they have not been able to lay an axe to it. The world
stands against it each day, but yet it grows. It is spreading
to every people group in every nation. It cannot stop
growing until all who will join have done so.

Do not lose heart when the kingdom of Satan opposes
you. The kingdom of God is prevailing. You are a part of
this powerful kingdom—a vine growing mighty in Me.

MARCH 15

I tell you, many will come from east and
west and recline at table with Abraham,
Isaac, and Jacob in the kingdom of heaven.

Matthew 8:11

❧

My kingdom is at once both inclusive and exclusive. People
from all walks of life and diverse people groups are invited,
but only those with humble hearts can gain entrance. This
is My way, and it is beyond the understanding of many.

The proud of heart cry out. They demand entrance to My
kingdom based on what they have done. They claim My
name over their deeds and bring this as evidence of their
fidelity to Me. They declare their works as righteous and
acceptable. But these follow the way of Cain in choosing
their religious practices over a true relationship with Me. I
send them away. They have no place in My kingdom
because their hearts do not belong to Me.

You have come to Me with a humble heart. You have put
on My robe of righteousness. I have welcomed you into My
kingdom. Remember always that you have a place at My
great feast table in heaven.

MARCH 16

The kingdom of heaven is like leaven that a woman took and hid in three measures of flour, till it was all leavened.

Matthew 13:33

৵৶

My kingdom is pervasive. By love, it spreads throughout the earth. It works silently, deep within the person. Heart by heart it moves as the Holy Spirit wills. One by one My Church grows.

Religion cannot stop My kingdom. Nations cannot snuff it out by edict or rules. Societies cannot dismiss it altogether. Cities and towns cannot contain its growth. Even families are powerless against its calling out of their members. Heart by heart, My kingdom moves and grows and lives and breathes. Soon, its time of spreading will be completed. Then, it will be time for My harvest.

I have called you to join Me in spreading My kingdom. It takes no special talent, just a heart willing to share My love with others. Enter into this great work today. I will show you how.

MARCH 17

*The kingdom of heaven is like treasure hidden in a field,
which a man found and covered up. Then in his joy he
goes and sells all that he has and buys that field.*

Matthew 13:44

❧

Each day, people come across My kingdom along the way.
Often they find it in the most unexpected of times and
places. But when they do, it is always the same—they hand
over their lives and everything they have in exchange for it.

Many look upon the salvation I offer in terms of what
they must give up. These wrestle with the pros and cons of
the cost required. I tell you, they will not find a cheap
bargain price. I require all that a person knows to give. I
then ask them for the rest of what they have as we walk the
path of sanctification together. Those who are wise gladly
hand over their worldly baubles for this heavenly treasure.
The foolish grasp tightly to what soon passes away. They
fail to acquire the treasure that never perishes.

Do not withhold any area of your heart from Me, My
child. I long to give you more of Me in exchange. You can
never have too much of Me. This is the way of the kingdom.

MARCH 18

*Again, the kingdom of heaven is like a merchant in
search of fine pearls, who, on finding one pearl of great
value, went and sold all that he had and bought it.*

Matthew 13:45-46

❧

Each day, people discover My kingdom as they search for
meaning in life. These may have some idea of what they are
looking for, but once they see the kingdom, they recognize
its worth and give everything in order to obtain entrance.

Mankind was created for fellowship with Me. Though sin
broke this fellowship, the spiritual hunger remained. Many
have filled this void with the things of the world. Still, they
hunger. Still, they search. What they seek, only I can
provide—a restoration of the fellowship between God and
mankind.

I created you to walk closely with Me. I long to share the
richness of My heart with you. Walk with Me. Give Me each
of your days, and you will receive more of Me in return.

MARCH 19

Again, the kingdom of heaven is like a net that was
thrown into the sea and gathered fish of every kind.
When it was full, men drew it ashore and sat down and
sorted the good into containers but threw away the bad.

Matthew 13:47-48

❧

My kingdom engages both those who will come in and those who will not. The gate into the kingdom is the dividing line between these two groups. I am the gate.

Much has been said about those who get into the kingdom, and rightly so. These celebrate My salvation forevermore. But I tell you, there are many, many more who do not get in. For these, My kingdom represents only judgment in the end, leading to eternal separation from Me.

Rejoice that you have been chosen and have responded to My voice! We will spend an eternity together. There will be no tears for those who did not come in. In My presence there is only joy.

MARCH 20

For the kingdom of heaven is like a master of a house who went out early in the morning to hire laborers for his vineyard. After agreeing with the laborers for a denarius a day, he sent them into his vineyard. And going out about the third hour he saw others standing idle in the marketplace, and to them he said, 'You go into the vineyard too, and whatever is right I will give you.' So they went. Going out again about the sixth hour and the ninth hour, he did the same. And about the eleventh hour he went out and found others standing. And he said to them, 'Why do you stand here idle all day?' They said to him, 'Because no one has hired us.' He said to them, 'You go into the vineyard too.'

Matthew 20:1-7

৵৩

I came to seek the lost and invite them into My kingdom. I am active in this pursuit, drawing these to Myself. At the hour they are found, they are prepared and sent into the work I have for them.

Some accept My invitation at an early age. These have a lifetime of walking with Me. Others may reject My call at first and only come to Me later in life. Some even come at the very hour of their death. Every one of these children is precious to Me. They have been bought with the same great price of redemption—My blood.

Walk with Me while you have the opportunity. Do the work I set before you with joy. Each day we journey together is priceless to Me, whether only for one day or for a lifetime full of days.

MARCH 21

And when evening came, the owner of the vineyard said to his foreman, 'Call the laborers and pay them their wages, beginning with the last, up to the first.' And when those hired about the eleventh hour came, each of them received a denarius. Now when those hired first came, they thought they would receive more, but each of them also received a denarius. And on receiving it they grumbled at the master of the house, saying, 'These last worked only one hour, and you have made them equal to us who have borne the burden of the day and the scorching heat.'

Matthew 20:8-12

❧❦

All who answer My call are granted eternal life. It does not matter when this happens in their lives. It is an equal reward for answering the same call. Admittance into My kingdom is a joyous occasion! Even the angels marvel and rejoice over each sinner who repents.

There are those I call to long years of difficult service. Their lives are marked with struggle and persecution. At the same time, others are given easier assignments for the kingdom. These live in places where I move freely or have assignments that flow readily along. Some have only a short time in this life and accomplish little for Me. Regardless of the length or nature of their service, all who answer My call are admitted into the kingdom.

If you have a lifetime to spend in My service, is it not better than just an hour? Think of all we can accomplish. Ponder how well we will know each other. Consider how much you can become like Me. And after all of this, think about how you will join Me in heaven where we will spend eternity together!

March 22

But he replied to one of them, 'Friend, I am doing you no wrong. Did you not agree with me for a denarius? Take what belongs to you and go. I choose to give to this last worker as I give to you. Am I not allowed to do what I choose with what belongs to me? Or do you begrudge my generosity?'

Matthew 20:13-15

❧

I am a just God. I deal uprightly with each of My children. I open heaven for those who come to Me early in life and those who come moments before they die. All who answer My call are welcomed into My kingdom.

The world scoffs at such an idea. It cannot see how this can be possible. Its people look with fleshly hearts, judging what is fair and what is not according to the ways of man. But justice comes from God alone. It is blind to all peripheral nuances and defines what is right and wrong from a perfect perspective.

When you get to heaven, you will be overcome with joy. You will be received with rejoicing and join in lifting up praise to the Most High God for paying the price of your admission. It is the same for all who have entered the kingdom, regardless of the circumstances.

MARCH 23

Then the kingdom of heaven will be like ten virgins who took their lamps and went to meet the bridegroom. Five of them were foolish, and five were wise. For when the foolish took their lamps, they took no oil with them, but the wise took flasks of oil with their lamps.

Matthew 25:1-4

છે્જ

Some day, I will come back for My children. I will know them because they have prepared themselves for that day. They are at peace with Me and their oil is full.

Many are not prepared for My return. Week after week they rush about their religious practices, thinking this will make them ready to meet Me. But they do not own the oil of a true relationship with Me. They are foolish, thinking mere association with My name or My people will earn them admittance into My kingdom. They confuse *participation* with *belonging.*

You are wise if your lamp shines with the fullness of a true relationship with Me. You are ready to meet Me however and whenever I come for you.

MARCH 24

As the bridegroom was delayed, they
all became drowsy and slept.

Matthew 25:5

❧◈❧

I have not yet returned for My children because the days of this age are not completed. I tell you, I may not come as soon as some believe, but I will come sooner than many believe.

There are those who say I will never return, that a day of reckoning—the separation of My sheep from the goats—is a myth. These sleep the slumber of foolishness, unconcerned with their eternal state. They reason in their hearts that if I were to come back, I would surely take them along with Me to heaven. These are mistaken. They are condemned in their foolishness. My children know better. Even though they may slumber while they wait, these know I am coming for them and expect to find them ready.

Prepare yourself for My return. You do not know the hour or day I will call you to Myself. Live each day in its fullness. Do all I ask of you while you wait. Do not become lulled into complacency!

MARCH 25

And while they [the foolish virgins] were going to buy [oil], the bridegroom came, and those who were ready went in with him to the marriage feast, and the door was shut. Afterward the other virgins came also, saying, 'Lord, lord, open to us.' But he answered, 'Truly, I say to you, I do not know you.'

Matthew 25:10-12

⊱⊰

I do not know the hour of My return for My children. Only My Father knows, and it is according to His plan. When it is time, He will send Me to gather My followers.

Who will I take with Me? Only those who have a true relationship with Me. These will enter into My marriage feast. It will be too late for the rest. They will have missed their final chance. Even though many will claim a lifetime in My service, I know they are imposters. They never *knew* Me. They only *knew of* Me.

You know Me because I know you. We will enter the marriage feast with gladness and rejoicing. You are so beautiful to Me!

MARCH 26

*The kingdom of heaven may be compared to a man who
sowed good seed in his field, but while his men were
sleeping, his enemy came and sowed weeds among the
wheat and went away. So when the plants came up and
bore grain, then the weeds appeared also.*

Matthew 13:24-26

৵৽

There are two kingdoms at work upon the earth—one is
Mine and the other belongs to Satan. These kingdoms are
set together in a spiritual struggle of good against evil. And
so it will be until the end.

Many confuse local church membership with
membership in My Church. They are not the same. My
Church contains only the members of My kingdom. The
local church contains members of both kingdoms engaged
side by side. In these churches, it is difficult to tell the
members of the two kingdoms apart. They look the same.
They do the same works. They even attach My name to
what they do. But I know who is Mine and who is not.

You are Mine. We both know this. Pray for My
discernment when working with others so you may see
whose kingdom they belong to. I tell you plainly, you will be
surprised at who belongs to My kingdom and who does not.

MARCH 27

*The field is the world, and the good seed is the sons of
the kingdom. The weeds are the sons of the evil one.*

Matthew 13:38

❧

The members of the two kingdoms are the sons and
daughters of the two kings. I know who are in both families,
as does Satan.

Most people ignore the reality of two families living upon
the earth. There are the sons and daughters of God, known
by their relationship with Me, and there are the sons and
daughters of Satan, who do not know Me. While the family
lines are quite distinct, neither group is bound to only good
or evil acts. Much good is done by the children of Satan in
the world, and much evil is done by the children of God.
For this reason, it can be difficult to tell the members of one
family from the other. Though human reasoning will fail in
this matter, I know the truth.

Do not be dismayed, My child, that there are weeds
growing in your midst. Do the works of your Father in
heaven, which I give to you. Bring glory only to Him.

MARCH 28

*The Son of Man will send his angels, and they will
gather out of his kingdom all causes of sin and all law-
breakers, and throw them into the fiery furnace. In that
place there will be weeping and gnashing of teeth.*

Matthew 13:41-42

৵৶

At the end of it all, I will gather Satan's children together.
Each will be judged by My words and their will. I will send
them into the lake of fire—the second death—which is a
just inheritance from their father. None will come into My
kingdom.

The world, which is under Satan's sway, proclaims that
no good God of love would do such a thing. But My Father
has given all judgment to Me, and I will judge each person
who does not belong to Me with righteous judgment. Once
judged, there will be no remedy.

My love for you keeps you far from such judgment.
Instead, you will enjoy an eternity with Me—the One you
have chosen.

MARCH 29

Then the righteous will shine like the sun in the kingdom of their Father. He who has ears, let him hear.

Matthew 13:43

❧

One day, all of My children will be gathered with Me to celebrate the love our Father has for us. In that day, there will be a celebration such as all of creation has never seen!

The destiny of My children is an eternity spent with Me. They will be celebrated as the sons and daughters of the Most High God. Every tear will be wiped away. They will shine forth like the sun, sharing in My glory. They will bow before the throne of God and rejoice in their salvation.

Know what awaits you, My child. You will enjoy your heavenly rewards for the rest of eternity as you assume the place and position you have earned while on earth. Remain steadfast until that day!

MARCH 30

The kingdom of God is as if a man should scatter seed
on the ground. He sleeps and rises night and day,
and the seed sprouts and grows; he knows not how.

Mark 4:26-27

૭ન્જી

I have called each of My children to do specific works in My kingdom. I have asked only that they do them faithfully in love and leave the results to Me.

Many take credit for the things I am doing in the world. These are proud of their efforts, supposing that the outcomes are due to their works. This could not be further from the truth! I work as I will in the world. I move as I see fit. I have My children participate so the world can see My power displayed through them. Those who have humble hearts know the truth. They see the miracles I perform and understand these are not the work of mere human hands.

Be faithful in the work I give you to do. Patiently plant and water as I instruct. It is My responsibility to bring forth the crop. I will do it in My timing.

MARCH 31

The earth produces by itself, first the blade, then the ear, then the full grain in the ear. But when the grain is ripe, at once he puts in the sickle, because the harvest has come.

Mark 4:28-29

୬ⴰ⭤

I am the Lord of the harvest. I cause your good deeds to produce fruit. The wise know and are glad. They labor joyously with Me as we bring in the harvest together.

The kingdom grows by the power of the Holy Spirit. He prepares the soil of the heart for the seed of truth so a bountiful harvest can be brought forth in My timing. No human can cause this to happen by their works or by their wills. No one can force the seed to grow. It is only by the Holy Spirit making Me known. *Sit quietly and consider what this means.*

Do not fret over the harvest, My child. Do not apply human reasoning to the process. Do your part and leave the result to Me. Then, rejoice greatly in what the Lord has done!

APRIL

Jesus is life. Apart from Him, there is no life.
Through Him, we obtain life. In Him, we truly live.

APRIL 1

For God so loved the world...

John 3:16

❧

I am the God of love. My love permeates the world in spite of the hate that evil spreads forth. I cause the sun to rise each day bringing its light and warmth. I bring rain to water the fields and forests, the meadows and the mountains. I do all of this and more without partiality to all the sons and daughters of man.

I know I am proclaimed as a God of hate in the world. Even within My Church, many see Me this way. I am presented as being prejudiced, exclusive, and angry. I am blamed for all that goes awry on this sin-damaged globe. But I tell you, the wise can see that these charges are false. They recognize My patience and mercy at work around them and in them. They know I am love.

I continue to extend My love to you each day. Look beyond the circumstances of your life and see it. Revel in its reality. Bask in its glow. Return it to Me with a grateful heart.

APRIL 2

...that he gave his only Son...

John 3:16

❧❧

Sacrifice. This is what your God has done. Coming in the flesh of mankind, I stepped down out of glory into the dust of the world. For you.

Mankind was in a hopeless state. Sin was the master and held all within its sway. The Law was given to show the way. The humble in heart knew they could not keep the perfection of the Law for even a day. They were doomed unless their God made a way for them. This is why I came among you as the perfect sacrifice to fulfill the requirements of the Law. My Father sent Me out of His great love for you. I am the gift of salvation for all who will believe.

Give to Me the sacrifice of your life—made possible by My sacrifice for you. I have walked upon the earth as men do. I now walk beside you as your God.

APRIL 3

*...that whoever believes in him should
not perish but have eternal life.*

John 3:16

༄༅

What I did was not done in secret. It was done plainly for all the world to see, so that in seeing, they might believe, and in believing, they might be saved.

The truth is there for all who will believe. The evidence is laid before the whole world. Its proof rests within the hearts of those who believe. It is borne out in their love for one another and their willingness to spread this love even to the unlovable. Whoever accepts this truth does not perish. Those who reject it are perishing already.

You have seen the truth of what I have done for you. You have come with a humble heart. You are no longer dead in your sins but are now made alive! Rejoice, My highly favored one. Rejoice!

APRIL 4

For God did not send his Son into
the world to condemn the world...

John 3:17

❧

I am the God of mercy. I extend My mercy to all in this life. I do not condemn them. My words and their wills condemn them. This way, they are without excuse.

I have shown mercy and love to each of My children. It is My desire that they extend the same to others around them. They are to be known by hearts full of love and mercy. But My Church has fallen prey to self-righteousness. They have forgotten who they once were and what they once did. They look at the world with condemning hearts. They judge the guilt of others while excusing their own. Their hatred is seen by the world and is condemned. I tell you, it is rightly condemned. *Where has My love gone?*

Remember who you once were. What is it that saved you from yourself? Extend this same mercy and love to those among you. It is not your place to condemn them. I will judge them in the end.

APRIL 5

...but in order that the world might be saved through him.

John 3:17

꙳

Only My love can heal a sin-sick heart. This is the love I brought into the world. By it, the Holy Spirit woos the heart and the sinner is saved.

As I have dealt with each of My children, I have shown them the way. It is the way of unconditional love given to the undeserving. This same key is to be used to open the hearts of others. It is an effective tool, full of My power. Yet, many try keys of their own making. All manner of emotional manipulation, threats, rules, regulations, traditions, and requirements are used to break open the locked hearts of sinners. But these are of little use. Love is *the* key.

How did I woo you to Myself? Was it not My unconditional love for you, poured out on the cross? This was the key that unlocked your heart. Use this love to unlock the hearts of others.

APRIL 6

Whoever believes in him is not condemned...

John 3:18

৵৶

My invitation is open to all. Even so, only those who will believe can escape the final condemnation at the end of the age. These will live eternally in My kingdom.

The *believing* I speak of is not a result of the application of some method. It is not found within any religious system. Man-made tradition is not its source. It cannot be inherited from a prior generation or transferred vicariously from another. It is not emotional or intellectual in nature. Instead, this belief is the convicting power of the Holy Spirit working in conjunction with a humble heart to produce faith. This is the powerful source of salvation's great work.

You have believed. You are numbered with the saints in My kingdom. You have escaped all condemnation—now and forevermore. *Understand what this means in your life.*

APRIL 7

...but whoever does not believe is condemned already, because he has not believed in the name of the only Son of God.

John 3:18

❧❧

Those who do not believe have condemned themselves. Truth is there to be seen, but they will not see it. All of My creation cries out to them, but they will not believe.

This is why I have told My children to stop judging others with an attitude of condemnation. It serves no purpose in My kingdom. They should know from their own experience that the only expectation to be made of a sinner is that they will continue to sin. Unless one has My new nature within them, it can be no other way. But I tell you, it is not their sinning that condemns them. It is their unbelief. *Those who have ears, let them hear!*

My child, let your heart be filled with compassion for the lost. They are sinners without the power to stop sinning. Do not condone their sin, but look past it with understanding. Do not condemn them, but give them the freedom to condemn themselves.

APRIL 8

*And this is the judgment: the light has come into
the world, and people loved the darkness rather
than the light because their works were evil.*

John 3:19

૭~ળ

I am the light shining in the dark world. My love is a beacon
sent out to those who are lost. My truth is a laser beam
precisely aimed at the falseness of the heart.

Evil seeks cover from the light of My truth. It prefers to
lurk in the darkness of deception were it cannot be seen. It
is here that it does its greatest work. Those who love evil
stay in the shadows. They will not come to the light because
light exposes the darkness of their hearts. In the light, their
works are judged by truth.

You are of the light. Walk in this light. Do not turn
toward darkness, but run from it. Turn to Me, and walk
with Me in the light. Darkness will be dispelled wherever we
go.

APRIL 9

For everyone who does wicked things hates the light and
does not come to the light, lest his works should be exposed.

John 3:20

୧୦୬

My light is the place of cleansing. It is the place of
righteousness. Forgiveness for every sin is found there. I
call all to come to the light so I can do My miraculous work
in their hearts.

I speak not only to the lost but also to My Church. Many
of My children hide in the darkness because they do not
want their secret sins exposed. Like Adam and Eve, they
seek to cover their deeds and hide from Me. By doing so, My
children refuse My forgiveness as surely as the wicked do.
Hiding from My truth, they forego My cleansing and are
imprisoned by their guilt. My power in their lives is
quenched, and their usefulness for My kingdom is blunted.
Yet, I walk upon the path and call out to them. I ask them
to leave their dark wickedness and come fully into My light
where forgiveness and restoration await.

You are of the light. Remain with Me in the light. Forsake
all double-mindedness and the sin that quickly entangles
you. Come to Me and receive forgiveness and cleansing.

APRIL 10

*But whoever does what is true comes to the
light, so that it may be clearly seen that his
works have been carried out in God.*

John 3:21

❧

My children are children of light. They shun the darkness
and its confusing ways. Instead, they bring their works to
Me in the light so My power behind these works can shine
forth.

My light is not a place of condemnation. It is a place of
forgiveness and approval. Those who expose their works to
the truth of My light see if what they have done is what I
have asked of them. In the light of My truth, My children
discern if it is their power behind the works or Mine. Those
who have worked according to My will see My approval.
Those who have worked in error must turn from their ways
so they can see My ready forgiveness.

You are of the light. Bathe in its cleansing power each
day, and do not fear it. This allows us to walk closely
together in approval and forgiveness. It is the way of all My
disciples.

APRIL 11

*Truly, truly, I say to you, unless one is born
again he cannot see the kingdom of God.*

John 3:3

∂∽∽

The kingdom of God is not of this world. It exists in the
world but lives apart from it. Flesh alone cannot enter the
kingdom. Efforts of the flesh cannot open its door. But I
have made a way.

Since the time of Adam, the sinful, fallen nature has
been passed down from each father to his children. I came
as the new Adam to make it possible for all of My children
to have a new nature—My nature. My Father, who is
sinless, passed this nature to Me as a human. I pass it to
each of My children when they are born again in Me. This
spiritual birth is a requirement for My kingdom, which is a
spiritual kingdom.

You have been born of the Holy Spirit. Your nature is
new. The old has been replaced. You now walk in the power
of My kingdom. Sin no longer has control over you. You
have been set free.

APRIL 12

Do not marvel that I said to you, 'You must be born again.'

John 3:7

❧

There is no mystery about the spiritual birth. Once you understand it is not of man but of the Holy Spirit, it can be taken for what it is.

Many have tried to explain away My requirement that all who will become My true followers must be born again. By removing the supernatural, they seek to make it a product of man's efforts. By relegating it to some kind of conscious awakening, they appeal to the pride of those who think they have discovered a higher plane of existence. The fact remains, though—this spiritual birth has nothing to do with man's power and everything to do with God's. It comes by divine intervention, not by human works.

You are My follower. You know the truth behind your spiritual birth. It was not of your doing but Mine. My love reached out to you, and you responded. I did the rest by the power of the Holy Spirit.

APRIL 13

Truly, truly, I say to you, unless one is born of
water and the Spirit, he cannot enter the kingdom
of God. That which is born of the flesh is flesh,
and that which is born of the Spirit is spirit.

John 3:5-6

❧⚬❧

My kingdom is spiritual in its essence. Flesh cannot pass from the physical world to the spirit world. Something must change.

Each of My children is born of the flesh. I mix the dust of the earth, give it a spirit, and breathe life into it. Later, when they are spiritually born, I add the Holy Spirit to their being, giving them a share in My eternal inheritance. From that moment on, I walk with them in the kingdom. My children begin their journey with Me on earth as flesh and continue it later in heaven as much more than flesh.

You are Mine. I celebrated each aspect of your life—from the time I created you in your mother's womb, to your physical birth, and on to your spiritual birth. Some day, I will bring you home to live with Me forever. It will be a day of great celebration!

APRIL 14

*The wind blows where it wishes, and you hear its sound,
but you do not know where it comes from or where it
goes. So it is with everyone who is born of the Spirit.*

John 3:8

৵৽

Who can explain the wind? Where does it come from? When
will it appear again? You can see its effects, but you cannot
see it. So it is with the Holy Spirit.

The Holy Spirit moves according to My Father's great
plan. Human effort cannot bring Him forth, no matter how
earnestly it is performed. People cannot control His
movement, regardless of how much they shout and
proclaim. Many will not accept this. They believe they can
command and manipulate the Holy Spirit, summoning Him
on demand to do their bidding. I tell you plainly, there are
many deceptions centered on the Holy Spirit, some from
man and some from the evil ones. The Holy Spirit moves
and makes Me known to those I am calling to the kingdom.
He moves only by the will of God.

The Holy Spirit made Me known to you. I called out to
you and you responded. Do not be deceived, but instead
pray for the Holy Spirit to work in your life, convicting you
when you sin, correcting you when you err, comforting you
during times of trial, and leading you into a greater
knowledge of Me. This is the true power of the Holy Spirit
working in your life.

APRIL 15

It is the Spirit who gives life; the flesh is no help at all.

John 6:63

❧❧

My truth must be spiritually discerned. It is the Holy Spirit who gives such discernment. Without this, you would be left to the confines of your flesh for understanding. While the mind has tremendous abilities, it also tends to create its own reality. You need the Holy Spirit to guide you into all understanding.

Mankind is very self-reliant. As the apex of My creation, humans are capable of much. But when it comes to spiritual understanding, they are lacking. This is why My Church is fractured and ineffective. Intellectual supposition has replaced wisdom. Philosophy has supplanted theology. Emotion regularly overrides truth. Fleshly thinking has spawned much error among My children, bringing confusion and needless complexity into My relationship with them.

Walk in the power of the Holy Spirit and you will not be deceived by the flesh. I intend for you to live by simple faith, not elaborate dogmas or religious traditions.

APRIL 16

Truly, I say to you, unless you turn and become like
children, you will never enter the kingdom of heaven.

Matthew 18:3

❧

The key to walking with Me into the kingdom is twofold—
turning and trusting. One must turn from their ways of
doing and thinking. Then, they must trust that My ways are
better.

People like to follow their own paths. They dream and
scheme their way through life, attempting to possess all
they want. Ulterior motives abound, clouding the thinking
and corrupting even what is good. My children are not
immune to acting independently from Me. That is why I give
them My mind and perspective—to help them die each day
to their desires and live to Mine.

Turn away from your independence! Come along with
Me. Leave behind all you are trusting in the world. This
place is temporary and unreliable. Put your hope in Me. I
am eternal and faithful. I love you and hold you in My
hand.

APRIL 17

Strive to enter through the narrow door. For many,
I tell you, will seek to enter and will not be able.

Luke 13:24

❧

I am the door. Only those who press forward urgently when called will enter into My kingdom. The rest will stand outside, shackled by their indecision and lack of commitment.

This is the great failing of modern religion—trying to crowd people into the kingdom without requiring a true commitment to Me. It is not easy to enter My kingdom. It demands a willingness to lay aside one's life for My sake. Such a decision is not convenient. It cannot be taken lightly. Many only want a Savior, not a Lord. I am both. These are My terms. They are non-negotiable for any who would enter My kingdom. Those who will not accept these terms will remain outside.

Decisively follow Me. Do not lose your sense of urgency. We have many things to do, and the time for doing them grows shorter each day. Much in your life with Me depends on this...both now and for all eternity.

APRIL 18

Enter by the narrow gate. For the gate is wide
and the way is easy that leads to destruction,
and those who enter by it are many.

Matthew 7:13

ॐॐ

There is a broad road in this life, and most people travel it. It requires little of the traveler, allowing them to do as they please and make their own way through life.

The wide gate is inviting. It swings easily on its hinges. It has room for the traveler and all of his or her ways. There seems to be no price for passing through. The road beyond looks smooth and easy as it disappears over the horizon. There are stops along the way to indulge the passions. The crowds move along in vast numbers. They are hopeful of their destination. It all seems very safe. But the end is not good for any who take this path. Many are dismayed when they discover it does not lead to My kingdom.

I rejoice that you have not chosen the broad path but have instead chosen Me. The narrow way is not easy. It has trials and tribulations. Nevertheless, I am with you at your side. I guide you to your final destination. Then, I receive you into eternal glory.

APRIL 19

For the gate is narrow and the way is hard that leads to life, and those who find it are few.

Matthew 7:14

❧

My way is the narrow path. It is entered with some effort through a narrow gate. The price of entry is your life given to Me in exchange for My life lived through you.

Many do not see the narrow gate as an option in this life. The cost of passing through it is too high. It seems very restrictive. It appears to eliminate many personal options. It looks difficult, spartan, and boring. Those who have passed through know better. The narrow gate leads to a life abundant with My presence. It opens to a path of infinite possibilities and opportunities. Along the way are broad vistas visible through My perspective. It is full of challenges, making boredom impossible. As we walk along, I provide every need for the journey.

I am excited that you have walked through the narrow gate! Take hold of My hand. I will never leave you or forsake you. We will walk together to the promised land.

APRIL 20

I am the door. If anyone enters by me, he will be saved and will go in and out and find pasture.

John 10:9

❧

There is only one doorway to heaven, and I am that door. I make it possible for My children to enter into the everlasting life of My kingdom.

Many of My children do not realize they will encounter other doors along the path of redemption we walk together. Some of these doors lead to the temporal distractions of the world. Others lead directly into realms of demonic control. All of them take My children off My path and put them on paths I never intended them to walk. Even so, I still work. I build bridges of mercy to bring them back from their wayward paths to Mine, from barren fields of strife to green pastures of peace.

You have chosen the best door. It has put you on the path of redemption. It leads to your destiny on earth and to your final destination, which is heaven. Do not open other doors along the way. They can lead to places of destruction in this life. *Listen and be wise.*

APRIL 21

I am the way...

John 14:6

❧

I cry out to all who will hear My voice. I stand in the marketplace. I search the byways. I walk throughout the entire earth seeking those who will respond to My call. *Come! This is the way!*

People the world over are searching, many without knowing exactly what they desire to find. Emptiness fills their souls—deep, dark caverns of yearning. They rush from one thing to the next, always seeking and never finding. Maybe the next relationship will satisfy or the next religious high. Perhaps more money or possessions will fill the bottomless void. On and on they go, and yet, they are empty. I call out to these, *I am the way!*

I am the way for you as well. Even after salvation, you have needs only I can meet. Bring these to Me. Do not substitute the things of the world. They cannot satisfy. Only I do.

APRIL 22

...[I am] the truth...

John 14:6

৵৵

Who can know what is true in this world? I can. Truth is the very expression of God. I am He. I am truth.

In the world, truth is subjective. It moves and breathes according to the whims of society and individuals alike. Cultures shape it and desires mold it. Everything is called into question and twisted—even the words I have spoken. Yet, mankind searches for truth each day. They need something to hold on to and believe in. I came to bring truth to a confused world...truth expressed in the very image of God in the flesh.

I am the highest expression of truth in your life. There is no confusion or shading of gray with Me. Get to know Me. You will see ever more clearly. I am who I am.

APRIL 23

...[I am] the life.

John 14:6

It is possible to be alive and yet not living. A beating heart signifies only mortal life. But what of spiritual life? How is this possible? Through Me. I am that spiritual life.

Many believe they are fully alive. They seize each day and take it captive to their wills. They toil and churn. They labor and sweat. They heap up earthly treasures and experiences for themselves. They step back and admire all they have done. Then they die, and what is the meaning of it all? I came to bring a better way—the way of life. Those who follow Me find significance in this life and glory in the next. They look back on a lifetime spent with Me and see they have truly lived. And it is only the beginning!

Many are the blessings of eternal life! You have already started the journey that is without an end. Physical death will not slow you down. You have been made spiritually alive in Me.

APRIL 24

No one comes to the Father except through me.

John 14:6

৯৩

My Father had a plan for you before the foundations of the world were laid. He watches you and waits for your arrival in heaven. I came to earth to make this possible.

It may seem that all is mere coincidence here on earth. This happens and then that. Leaders rise and nations fall. Toil and strife follow rest and peace. But I tell you, the world is being drawn relentlessly toward a final conclusion. One day, the full plan of My Father will be fulfilled. All who have come to Him will share in His eternal glory. This is why I came to earth two thousand years ago—to make a way for those who would believe in Me to go to My Father in heaven.

My Father loves you. He takes special interest in all you do. He waits patiently for you to finish your tasks on earth so you can be received into heaven. Then, you will join with all of the saints in singing praise to Him.

APRIL 25

...since you have given him [Jesus] authority over all flesh,
to give eternal life to all whom you have given him.

John 17:2

❧

My Father chose you before time began. He sent Me to make a way for you, followed by the Holy Spirit to draw you to Me. You were chosen so you could choose Me. I could then give you eternal life.

Some struggle with the idea that there are people who the Father chose for eternal life even before the world was made. Others wrestle with the idea that each man or woman is free to willfully choose or reject Me when they are called. Listen to Me when I tell you that both are true. The chosen are called by the Holy Spirit and enabled to understand who I am and all I offer to them. They must then choose. Those who will choose Me are given to Me by My Father, and I give them eternal life. Those who reject Me are pursued. If they die in their rejection, they die in their sins.

You were chosen before the earth was formed. The Holy Spirit called, and you answered. I have given you eternal life. Thank your Father in heaven for choosing you, one out of the many.

APRIL 26

And this is eternal life, that they know you, the only
true God, and Jesus Christ whom you have sent.

John 17:3

❧

It is important who you know in this life. If you do not know
the Father through the Son by the power of the Holy Spirit,
you cannot share in eternal life.

Man is forever busy with his religion. There is no end to
his devoted practices. But heaven cannot be gained by
religion. No number of good works is sufficient to pay for an
entrance. Eternal life is possible only by way of a living
relationship with the one true God. This relationship can
only come through Me, His Son, as the Holy Spirit draws.
There is no other way.

You are loved by all of us—the Father, Son, and Holy
Spirit. You were chosen and are known by us. *It is*
marvelous, don't you agree?

APRIL 27

All that the Father gives me will come to me, and
whoever comes to me I will never cast out.

John 6:37

છે;

Eternal life is a permanent possession. It is not earned, nor is it deserved. It is given as a gift. Those who receive it cannot lose it.

Some of My children have been taught that My salvation is conditional and depends on them. They live their days without the peace of knowing they are truly Mine. They see Me as a merciless God who watches their every move, looking for a reason to revoke their eternal life. These have been taught in error and are kept in bondage by those who will one day give an account to Me. I tell you, whoever is made Mine will never lose their place in My kingdom. They have been bought by My blood and are My eternal heirs. Nothing can snatch them out of My hand.

Do not fear! Your salvation depends on what I have done, not on what you will do. Enter into My rest and rejoice!

APRIL 28

*For this is the will of my Father, that everyone who
looks on the Son and believes in him should have
eternal life, and I will raise him up on the last day.*

John 6:40

❧

My Father's plan is perfect. No deficiencies are found with
it. He pursues it with flawless precision. His harvest is
priceless.

What can man say about My Father's plan? Will he find
fault? As he looks at the motive, will he see anything but
love? As he examines the method, will he not find mercy?
When he observes the means, will he not discover justice?
Many find fault with My Father. They question His
character and the nature of His attributes. They diminish
His relevance in the affairs of the world. They reject His
demand that a final account must be given for every life
lived. Such people are fools who have been given over to
their foolishness. On the day of judgment, they will feel the
sting of His perfect justice.

Sit quietly before your God and consider His ways. Look
to His plan for mankind's salvation. Marvel at its perfect
simplicity. Think about His relentless pursuit of you leading
to your salvation. *Be still and know that He is God.*

APRIL 29

You search the Scriptures because you think that in them you have eternal life; and it is they that bear witness about me, yet you refuse to come to me that you may have life.

John 5:39-40

કરન્જી

From Genesis to Revelation, My Word cries out. In these pages of Scripture you can find life because you can find Me.

I have given My Word to the world. I have guarded it throughout the centuries. It is now instantly accessible in a multitude of languages. It has much to say about Me. Yet, My Word is a puzzle to those who are not being drawn by the Holy Spirit. These cannot see the truth of who I am and what I have done. To them, it is not believable.

I have given you My Word, and you have the Holy Spirit. The words of Scripture are life. Read and understand. Seek to know Me more.

APRIL 30

For the Son of Man came to seek and to save the lost.

Luke 19:10

❧

All of mankind was once lost. By My love, some are now found in the kingdom. This continues until the last day. I cannot stop before all has been accomplished. It is why I have come.

My children, do not grow weary of doing the things I have called you to do. If I, your Master, continue in My work upon the earth, why would you not also expect to do the same? However, I do not want you to be busy for the kingdom, as is the habit of those who do works according to what they believe is right. Instead, I want you to be productive. This is possible by listening to Me and doing *only* what I ask of you. Remember, I am the One who saves the lost. The best you can do is to love them as I have loved you—in mercy and truth. Together, we will accomplish what must be done for the kingdom. It will grow as I will it to grow.

Let us be about My work in the kingdom. Do not get ahead of Me in the work. Do not carry burdens that are not yours to carry. Remain at My side and see what great things will be done.

MAY

Jesus showed us the nature of kingdom living. It is based on His love and His mercy. It digs deep past all the fluff to the very motives of the heart. It goes the extra mile.

MAY 1

*Blessed are the poor in spirit, for
theirs is the kingdom of heaven.*

Matthew 5:3

❧

The citizens of My kingdom are humble. They do not think
more highly of themselves than they should. They know
they are the sons and daughters of God, but they are keenly
aware of why this is the case.

The world is not a humble place. Its foundation is pride.
Its people are desperate to feel they are special. They chase
after any person, place, or possession that validates their
worth. They elevate themselves through endless self-
promotion. They lord over those they can. Many of My
children have fallen into this same trap of the world. They
have confused *self-worth* with *self-value*. Have they
forgotten that, despite who they once were, I chose to love
them unto death?

You are My precious child. Because I love you, you have
great value. I do not judge your worth as the world does. I
look at the great work I am doing in your heart. You are
priceless!

MAY 2

Blessed are those who mourn, for they shall be comforted.

Matthew 5:4

❧

All of My children fail Me. Despite their best efforts, they stumble and fall. I am always there to pick them up in their repentance.

The way of the world is to excuse one's sin. Its people seek to cover their feelings of shame by overlooking their failures and pointing out the faults of others. Much of their sin is celebrated and made socially acceptable. How many of My children have adopted this same approach? How many seek self-acceptance at the expense of others, looking to salve their consciences by comparing the relative seriousness of sins? I tell you plainly, I see all sin as the same—an offense against the Most High God!

Do not hide your sin. Instead bring it to Me and mourn over it. Turn from it, and I will forgive you. Then we will continue our walk together through the kingdom.

MAY 3

Blessed are the meek, for they shall inherit the earth.

Matthew 5:5

❦

I ask all of My children to practice meekness while they wait for the time My kingdom is complete. They will be rewarded with the inheritance of days without end.

The world celebrates power and might. It seeks to dominate and control. It takes advantage of those it can by the force of violence or by the laws of its governments. It ridicules all who are brought to weakness and stands over them defiantly. My Church has become hostile to such treatment. It seeks to have its way in the world and to be on equal footing. My people have forgotten that this has never been the case, nor will it ever be. They have forgotten My words to them about being persecuted. They have forgotten that even I, their Master and King over all, was unjustly subjected to the hatred of the world and endured it, even to death.

Do not look to avoid the persecutions that come with being My follower. Patiently endure your temporary state of suffering. The day is coming when you will join Me to celebrate the end of this world and its troubles. Until then, be about the work of My kingdom in love.

MAY 4

Blessed are those who hunger and thirst for
righteousness, for they shall be satisfied.

Matthew 5:6

❧

My righteousness is just and true. It is built upon love. My disciples seek it and allow it to permeate their lives, conforming them to My likeness.

The world practices only self-righteousness. Its people seek to set their own standards of purity and justice. To them, everything is relative. They have no thirst for My righteousness, which they see as too constraining. My children are not immune to such thinking. Many are adept at the practice of self-righteousness. They condemn others based on their personal standards, which are not just or true. They think more highly of themselves than they should. They forget that it is no great feat to find someone more evil than they are.

Seek My righteousness and not your own. Let this be the mirror by which you evaluate yourself. It will assist you in your quest to remain humble and usable for My kingdom.

MAY 5

Blessed are the merciful, for they shall receive mercy.

Matthew 5:7

༚

I am the God of mercy and grace. I patiently deal with the sons and daughters of man. My mercy reaches out across the entire world so all might see My love.

The world places little value on mercy. Its people are always striving and grasping. Those who stand in the way are callously thrust aside. The end always justifies the means. Likewise, some of My people have lost their sense of mercy. They collect injustices inflicted upon them and lock forgiveness away in their hearts. They allow ambition and pride to blind them to the human casualties left in their wakes. They become uncaring in the face of suffering, their hearts hardened and pitiless.

Great mercy and graciousness I have shown to you! It is renewed and refreshed every morning. Consider any from whom you are withholding forgiveness. Think of those around you who are in need of mercy today. Go and forgive them. Go and touch them with My love.

MAY 6

Blessed are the pure in heart, for they shall see God.

Matthew 5:8

☞❦

I am holy and I am pure. My love is the same. It is single-minded in its purpose. It is unconditional in its expression.

The world is a place of hidden motives. Actions are not what they seem. Words kindly spoken carry snares. Manipulation lurks in every interaction. This is the way of man. The source is the heart. Because of this, I call each of My children to allow the Holy Spirit to purify their heart. How can you love others unconditionally if your heart is not pure? How can you serve faithfully without complaint? How can you give and expect nothing in return? Only from a pure heart are these acts possible.

Give Me your heart. Allow Me to cleanse it. Let Me turn it from stone to flesh and make it alive by the Holy Spirit. Then, you will begin to see Me clearly as I walk beside you along the way.

MAY 7

Blessed are the peacemakers, for
they shall be called sons of God.

Matthew 5:9

৵৵

I call all of My children to be peaceable in their dealings
with others. This is not the peace of capitulation or
compromise. It is the peace of tolerance, patiently extended
in love.

The world is a place of oppression where arrogance rules
from prideful hearts. Little room is found for opposing
views. Forcefulness is seen as a virtue and power as a
necessity. The tone is anti-God and the spirit is anti-Christ.
I have placed My Church in the midst of this hostile world
to demonstrate My love to those who are unlovable. Some
have allowed religion to hijack My message and turn it into
a battle for the cultures around them. This war is waged
with an equal amount of hate and disdain on both sides. I
tell you plainly, this is not My way. My children only need
to look at the example I left them...and My peace.

I have given you My peace for the trials you face in this
life. I have given you My message of love to carry to the
world. You are My ambassador to the nations. Represent
Me well!

MAY 8

*Blessed are you when people hate you and when
they exclude you and revile you and spurn your
name as evil, on account of the Son of Man!*

Luke 6:22

৵৵

I have plainly warned all of My followers to expect trouble in
the world. It is not possible for it to be otherwise with those
who truly follow Me and do as I ask. But there is a
difference between being persecuted for what one does and
being persecuted for My sake. *Stop for a moment and
consider all that this means for your life.*

The world is at continual war with Me. It hates Me and
despises My call to salvation. But I have already won the
war. So now, the world has turned its attention to My
followers. The same spirit that hates Me hates them. Yet I
have called them to stand in the face of this onslaught.
Some of My children stand well. They go where I lead and
do what I ask. These are persecuted for My sake. Others,
though, go their own way. They provoke opposition
needlessly because they do not follow where I lead or do
what I ask. These suffer persecution for their own sakes.

You will have trouble with the world when you follow Me.
Those who hate Me will hate you. They will persecute you,
perhaps even unto death. Yet, I will be with you and help
you to endure to the end.

MAY 9

Rejoice in that day, and leap for joy, for behold, your reward
is great in heaven; for so their fathers did to the prophets.

Luke 6:23

❧

Those who are persecuted for My sake pile up great rewards
in heaven. These treasures are safely kept for them until
the day of their arrival. On that day, I present them to My
children with great delight.

Joy in the midst of persecutions is not a work of the
flesh. It is only possible by the Holy Spirit working within
you. The flesh seeks to escape all discomfort as quickly as
possible. But those who walk by the Holy Spirit have My
strength to endure the trial with great hope. They do not
turn to the left or the right but walk through the trial set
before them. These see My affirming love for them in the
midst of the persecutions and know they will soon be
gathered to Me forever in glory.

My child, rejoice when you are persecuted because you
are doing what I have asked of you. See it as a confirmation
that you are closely following Me into the great spiritual
battle that rages around you. I am adding to your treasures
in heaven while using your testimony of faithfulness on
earth.

MAY 10

*But woe to you who are rich, for you have
received your consolation. Woe to you who are
full now, for you shall be hungry. Woe to you
who laugh now, for you shall mourn and weep.*

Luke 6:24-25

࿇

Eternal treasures are lasting. They do not fade with one's
life here on earth but are enjoyed forevermore. They are a
reflection of the heart, signifying the priority of a life lived
before Me. *Let the wise heed these words.*

The world celebrates richness and fullness and laughter.
Its way is the way of the present moment. It forsakes the
future for the enjoyment of the *now.* Many of My children
have bought into this lie. They listen intently to the cry of
their flesh. They are not interested in the discomfort of
being poor in spirit. They reject the sacrifice of hungering
and thirsting after Me. They want no part of humbling
themselves and mourning their sins. These have only the
rewards of such actions to enjoy in this present world. Their
treasure room is empty in heaven.

You have been chosen for My service in this life. Your
rewards await you in heaven. Daily you add to your great
pile of treasure as you walk with Me.

MAY 11

Woe to you, when all people speak well of you,
for so their fathers did to the false prophets.

Luke 6:26

৵৵

Do not seek favor with the world. Instead, walk through it in the light of My truth with love and mercy. The world is not your home. Its favors come at a great price to you.

The world despises My truth and hates those who walk by it. It has always been this way, and so it will be until the end. The world only accepts those who come on its terms. It only loves those who hate Me. Yes, the world gives the impression of accepting the good deeds of those who are Mine, but underneath their shallow display of flattery is a deep loathing of the source of this good. Some of My children have become friends with the world. They seek its acceptance, and they bask in its accolades. I tell you, they have been deceived and have become false. They are loved by the world only because they have left their first love.

I love you. I am your first and greatest love. Humbly approach the world with My love and mercy, but do not become its friend. Grant its people the respect due to them as fellow humans. Always be aware, though, that the world *remains* at war with Me and all who follow Me.

MAY 12

You are the salt of the earth, but if salt has lost
its taste, how shall its saltiness be restored? It
is no longer good for anything except to be
thrown out and trampled under people's feet.

Matthew 5:13

ॐॐ

My truth is salty. It flavors and it preserves. It creates a thirst in all who will consider it, one I am ready to satisfy.

I have placed My people specifically all over the earth. Each of them carries My truth in their hearts. This truth is meant as a flavoring for all they touch. It affects their speech and their actions. It can be found in the very attitudes of their hearts. For those of My children who allow it, My truth will preserve them in all situations with its eternal perspective. But just as salt can lose its flavor, My truth can lose its edge. The cares of this world and the temporal affections of the heart can blunt its impact. Soon, it is so dulled that the philosophies of the world mix easily with it, making it useless. Those who were once guided by truth become awash in a sea of confusion.

Guard your heart carefully. Allow the truth I have deposited there to grow and flow out to those around you. Let it season every interaction—not in a heavy-handed, overpowering way but in practiced doses that reflect My way with others.

MAY 13

You are the light of the world. A city set on a hill
cannot be hidden. Nor do people light a lamp and put
it under a basket, but on a stand, and it gives light to
all in the house. In the same way, let your light shine
before others, so that they may see your good works
and give glory to your Father who is in heaven.

Matthew 5:14-16

কৈৎ

My truth is light. It shines in a dark world so others may
see it and be drawn to Me.

Each of My children is a bearer of My light. As they allow
it, I shine forth from their hearts. Others see this light and
are drawn to it. As this light shines in the dark, I do My
work in the hearts of those I will. It is possible for My
followers to so dim My light that it becomes washed out by
other beacons shining from the world. Those who allow this
to happen cannot be used to attract others to Me. They lack
the light necessary to illuminate even their own way in the
darkness. Their works for Me are weak and few. These go
unnoticed in the busy world around them. They lose their
opportunity to bring glory to their Father in heaven.

You bear the light of My truth in your heart. Let it shine
forth with intense love and mercy to those around you. This
allows Me to give you works to do beyond your capacity and
capability so others can clearly see the true source of your
works and lift up praise to our Father.

MAY 14

You have heard that it was said to those of old, 'You shall not murder; and whoever murders will be liable to judgment.' But I say to you that everyone who is angry with his brother will be liable to judgment; whoever insults his brother will be liable to the council; and whoever says, 'You fool!' will be liable to the hell of fire.

Matthew 5:21-22

❧

I look into the heart, past the surface actions. I consider the emotions and attitudes behind every thought, word, and deed. *When I look at yours, what do I see?*

The world is an angry, hate-filled place. Murder is found in the hearts of its people. These hurl insults and then laugh. They treat the feelings and wellbeing of others with little regard. Some of this anger has crept into My Church. My own people do not practice My love for one another. They bicker and struggle with others who do not see things the same way as they do. Hate lies behind their attitudes and actions as surely as it lies behind murder. The world observes and calls My Church to account. They do not see My love within, and they do not experience it without.

I created a new heart within you, one built up in My love. Let this love be shared with others. Be quick to hear, slow to speak, and slow to become angry. This way, all will know you are My disciple.

MAY 15

So if you are offering your gift at the altar and there remember that your brother has something against you, leave your gift there before the altar and go. First be reconciled to your brother, and then come and offer your gift.

Matthew 5:23-24

☙❧

I am the God of forgiveness. I am full of mercy and unconditional love. I do not desire your religious practices. Instead, I seek a heart that is humble and pure.

Unforgiveness is a serious sin. Its root is pride. Its fruits are hatred and bitterness. Though the world has long practiced this base trait of mankind, it should not be found within My Church. Instead, My people should be characterized by forgiveness. After all, have I not forgiven much of each of My children? Do I not continue to forgive them day after day after day? How, then, can any of them refuse to forgive?

Do not take My forgiveness of your trespasses lightly. Be thankful and rejoice greatly! Offer this same gift to those who have offended you, both in My Church and in the world. By this, My love is multiplied.

MAY 16

You have heard that it was said, 'You shall not commit adultery.' But I say to you that everyone who looks at a woman with lustful intent has already committed adultery with her in his heart.

Matthew 5:27-28

৵৵৽

Mankind is created in the image of God. When I did this, it was My intention that every man and woman would become an image bearer, carrying the likeness of their God into the world in the form of a spiritual being walking in a physical body. Because love is the essence of the Godhead, love would likewise be the hallmark of mankind.

After man sinned, the concept of image bearing became twisted in the world. People began to look upon one another as physical beings, and love was redefined as an emotion based on physical attraction. In this changed world, the sensual replaced the spiritual. And it is here that My children must contend with their view of other people. Will it be as My image bearers or as common beasts of the field?

I hold you in high regard. I made you to carry the very image of God in the world. Do not regard others as less than this. Value them as I value them. Treat them as I would also treat them.

MAY 17

If your right eye causes you to sin, tear it out and throw it away. For it is better that you lose one of your members than that your whole body be thrown into hell. And if your right hand causes you to sin, cut it off and throw it away. For it is better that you lose one of your members than that your whole body go into hell.

Matthew 5:29-30

❧

As My child, My power is yours for the asking. Where you are weak, I can make you strong. Even so, I expect you to act wisely by removing those things in your life that entangle you and cause you to stumble and fall.

The world is about the lust of the eyes, the lust of the flesh, and the pridefulness of man. Yet, each of My children must journey through this life and engage the world around them. Many who decide to follow Me try to do it on their terms. As we walk together, they are not willing to let go of the *very same* things that defined them as sinful people before I came into their lives. Instead, they try to walk with one foot on My path while seeing how close they can get to their old ways with the other foot. I tell you, these will fail because of their double-mindedness.

Walk with Me on the path I have chosen for you. Let go of the things of the world that quickly entangle you and cause you to stumble. You know what they are. I have told you. *Will you listen?*

MAY 18

Again you have heard that it was said to those of old, 'You shall not swear falsely, but shall perform to the Lord what you have sworn.' But I say to you, Do not take an oath at all, either by heaven, for it is the throne of God, or by the earth, for it is his footstool, or by Jerusalem, for it is the city of the great King. And do not take an oath by your head, for you cannot make one hair white or black. Let what you say be simply 'Yes' or 'No'; anything more than this comes from evil.

Matthew 5:33-37

❧❧

My disciples are known by the strength of their character. They say what they mean and do what they say. They do not rely on the quantity of their words or the volume of their voices in making their intentions known.

The world is filled with boastfulness. People contend by way of impressive speeches and proud expressions. They verbally thrust and parry, seeking the upper hand. The intent behind their words is to gain something at the expense of others. They give evidence of their earnestness and trustworthiness by swearing on things even more impressive than their arrogance. I remind My children that sin lurks in the multitude of their words. The wise hear and speak the truth plainly and simply. They have nothing to hide, so their words can be trusted without enhancement. The power behind their speech is a lifetime of truthfulness.

I look into your heart to discern your intent. I listen to hear if your words match your heart. I rejoice as truthfulness reigns, when there is no shadow of turning and twisting for advantage. I see you as a person of your word, speaking with a steadfast heart. Whatever you say, I look for you to do.

MAY 19

You have heard that it was said, 'An eye for an eye and a tooth for a tooth.' But I say to you, Do not resist the one who is evil. But if anyone slaps you on the right cheek, turn to him the other also.

Matthew 5:38-39

৵৵৻

The humble in heart seek to express My love and mercy with great patience. These do not look for ways to retaliate for personal slights but instead try to emulate Me in the midst of a lost and dying world.

When the world pushes, it expects a push back. When it insults, it expects the same in return. When it causes hurt, it steels itself for retribution. Such is its way and the way of its people. I call My children to walk differently. Just as I have tolerated the ungracious ways of My own toward Me, I call them to absorb the unkindness of the world around them with patient endurance. It is no great thing to return hate for hate, but returning love for hate is a sign that the Holy Spirit is alive and at work in one's life. The world will see this and stand in amazement.

Allow the Holy Spirit to have His way within you so your first reaction will be patience instead of anger and love instead of hate. By this, you make My power within you come alive, and you become a marvelous testimony to all who see it.

MAY 20

And if anyone would sue you and take your tunic,
let him have your cloak as well. And if anyone
forces you to go one mile, go with him two miles.

Matthew 5:40-41

❧

Part of laying down your life for Me is laying down your
personal rights. For how can you hold tightly to your rights
while you release your life? Personal rights are
entitlements. These create expectations and limit what I
can do with your life.

The world places a high value on rights. It is forever
wrangling over perceived insults against one group or
another. Yet, how quickly it turns and violates the rights of
others for the sake of its own! My people are many times
the focus of such violations. They are mistreated. They are
inconvenienced and taken advantage of. They are insulted
and maligned. Know that this is the spirit of antichrist at
work. It is alive in the world and will be so until the end.
Such evil does not discriminate. It opposes all who belong
to Me. In its midst, I call My children to reflect My love, not
considering themselves above the One whom they have
pledged to serve.

I have called you out of the darkness of the world and
into My light. You can now see clearly the ways of darkness.
Do not be dismayed! Instead, be wise in your perspective
and longsuffering in your endurance. In this way, the
others I am calling out of the same darkness can see My
light in you.

MAY 21

Give to the one who begs from you, and do not refuse the one who would borrow from you.

Matthew 5:42

❧

I have loved you unconditionally, expecting nothing in return. I have given of My power, knowing you could not do what I have asked without it. I have shared the truths of My kingdom, replacing your opinions and philosophies. I have handed My abundance to you because you lacked resources for our walk.

As I have given to you, you are to give to others as I direct your hands to do so. Give to those who cannot repay you in the same way as you give to those who can—expecting nothing in return. In so doing, you show the world a better way than its constant grasping and favor-mongering. By your willingness to do what I ask of you in this regard, you will experience My joy in your life and see it spread to the lives of others. They will be drawn to the light in you.

I have given to you so you can give to those I choose to bless from your hand. Whether out of your abundance or want, the joy that accompanies giving in My name will be yours. So give as I lead, expecting nothing in return. This will be a great blessing to others and to you.

MAY 22

And as you wish that others would do to you, do so to them.

Luke 6:31

❧

I have given you a better way to live. Instead of merely asking you to refrain from doing something negative to those around you, I have commanded you to do something positive—love them in the same way you love yourself.

All of mankind shares the desire for love, respect, and acceptance as human beings. These are the basic building blocks of human dignity. It is the way of the world to demand these with little thought of giving them in return. Such is the way of all lovers of self. My way is different. It is the way of empathy and selflessness. As My children look within themselves to see how they desire to be dealt with as human beings, I command them to treat others the same way. By doing so, My followers are constantly reminded to demonstrate My love to those who come across their paths each day.

You are a child of My unconditional love. Think about how you want to be treated. Go out and extend these same courtesies to others.

MAY 23

If you love those who love you, what benefit is that to you?
For even sinners love those who love them.

Luke 6:32

❧

I give love to those who are unlovable. I expect nothing in return. I choose to love them even if they reject Me time after time and push Me away year after year. Many of My children came to Me only after years of My calling out to them. These know the wonder of a pursuing love.

The world loves those who love it. It gives love so it may receive love in return. It does not know how to love without a motive. Even its practice of *paying it forward* asks the recipient to go and do likewise. This is not a love free of conditions but one of motives and compulsion. I call My children to love those I lead them to. I ask them to put aside their aspirations for this love and to leave the result with Me. Motive-free love is unconditional love. It is loving others simply because I have asked.

You have a great capacity for love because you have experienced the power of unconditional love in your life. You know how this type of love tears down the defensive walls and allows the Holy Spirit to flow through the interaction. As you love others this way, you make room for Me to work.

MAY 24

*And if you do good to those who do good to you, what
benefit is that to you? For even sinners do the same.*

Luke 6:33

❧

If you do good for your sake, your reward is of this world,
temporary and fleeting. If you do deeds for My sake, your
reward is laid up in heaven. It is everlasting.

Many make it a practice to *give to get*. In doing so, their
true motive is to gain something for their good deed—
recognition, satisfaction, congratulation, adoration, or
compensation. Even My children get caught in this
deception. They are told to do good things for Me so I will
reward them. They are told to give their money so I can out-
give them. But doing things—whether good or even in My
name—to get something from Me in return is not My way. I
see it as nothing less than an attempt to manipulate Me.
Stop and consider this.

I long to give you every good thing for your life. I don't
need to be bribed to do so. Follow Me with a pure heart.
Serve Me only from your love for Me. See what happens
when you do!

May 25

And if you lend to those from whom you expect to receive, what credit is that to you? Even sinners lend to sinners, to get back the same amount.

Luke 6:34

❧

Do not lend to others. Instead, freely give as I direct. Lending has obligatory strings attached. These strangle those who receive and keep them in bondage to the lender. Giving freely comes without expectations for you, the giver, or for the person who receives. It is a true blessing for both parties.

Lending money may seem charitable, but it is not. It is not a good work because it creates an obligation and is a form of bondage. Giving is a good work. There is no expectation of repayment. Both parties can give thanks— the giver, because I have provided the means, and the receiver, because I have blessed them in their time of need. This type of giving is done out of love—for Me and for those who receive what is given. It is part of My economic policy in the world.

I give to you so you may give to others. I look for a multiplying, not a hoarding. I give freely without interest or expectation of repayment. I then allow you to be My conduit of blessing to those in need. Great is the joy of giving! Receive from Me with an open hand, and be ready to pass My blessing along.

MAY 26

And if you greet only your brothers, what more are you
doing than others? Do not even the Gentiles do the same?

Matthew 5:47

❧

I extended My hand of friendship to you while you were yet
a sinner. Now that you are in My kingdom, I call you to
reach out to others who are sinners. In the same way I did
not withhold My hand because of your lifestyle and choices,
so I command you to not withhold your hand from those to
whom you are sent.

My people tend to cluster together for safety. In fear,
many build fortresses on earth to shut out selected
influences from the world. I tell you plainly, it is not
possible to do this without shutting out the world itself. I
did not call you to isolation but spread you throughout the
earth so the world would clearly see My love at work. I did
not ask you to be a saltbox that only stores salt but a
saltshaker so you could season the world as you walk
through it. I did not ask you to bottle up My love and
extend it only to each other but to let it flow freely to those
around you. This is My way for you—to be in the world but
not of it, to be light dispelling the darkness while not
becoming dissipated by it.

Do not shy away from the assignments I give to you. Go
where I send you. Do not be surprised by the life choices of
others. Love them with mercy, and watch to see what I will
accomplish.

MAY 27

But love your enemies, and do good, and
lend, expecting nothing in return...

Luke 6:35

৵৵

Enemies will rise up against you. Some will be of your own
making, and some will come forth because of Me. No enemy
can be turned to Me by force. By love, though, some can be
overcome.

Every person can be known by their enemies, for by
them, one knows what that person stands for. Those of My
children who follow Me will have enemies from the world
and from within My Church. The world will not stand idly
by as My disciples conduct kingdom business. Likewise,
many in My Church will rise up against those who shake off
the shackles of their religious ways and begin to walk as I
lead. In both cases, an opponent is created when their way
of life is made uncomfortable by My truth. Though these
adversaries try to force compromise through ridicule,
exclusion, threats, and even violence, their hatred must not
be returned. Instead, these enemies must be loved through
actions and brought to Me in prayer so I can deal with them
as I may.

I have given you My peace in the world. Do not return
hurt for hurt upon your adversaries. Instead, be peaceable.
Turn them over to Me so I can work things out for your
ultimate good.

MAY 28

*...and your reward will be great, and
you will be sons of the Most High...*

Luke 6:35

❧

My children can heap up rewards for themselves in heaven.
All they must do is walk with Me, going where I send them
and doing what I instruct them to do. Such is the way of
kingdom living.

Rewards are given by their keeper. My children choose
the keeper by their actions. Those who do the things I have
instructed lay up treasures in heaven. These gifts are Mine
to give. They are eternal and do not fade with the passing of
life on earth. Those who go their own way and do what they
think is best, lay up treasures on earth. These come from
the evil one to confuse the foolish and keep them from
doing as I ask. These rewards are temporary and soon pass
from the hands of the receiver. You cannot serve two
masters. Either you serve Me, or you serve Satan who is
against Me. By your choice, you will receive your reward
from the one you serve.

Build eternal treasures while you journey upon the
earth. It gives Me great pleasure to give them to you and
keep them for you until your arrival in heaven. Your earthly
life is like a puff of smoke. What you gain here is soon lost
forever. What you gain in heaven, you will enjoy throughout
eternity.

MAY 29

*...for he [the Most High God] is kind
to the ungrateful and the evil.*

Luke 6:35

❧⚜❧

My Father in heaven allows good things to be taken from
His children and given to the sons and daughters of men.
He does this so My followers can be made more like Me in
both their joys and their sorrows. He also knows that these
who do good—even to their own hurt—will be known as His
own sons and daughters upon the earth.

I have not asked you to treat others any differently than
My Father does. He is patient and kind to those on earth,
even when they are ungrateful and evil. Because of this,
these are left without an excuse on the final day of
judgment. He is love. He is just. He will not forget His
children on that day.

You are ever on the mind of God. You are watched with
great anticipation. You are cheered on at every step along
the way. Soon, the day of reckoning will come, and every
account will be set straight. On that day, I tell you, you will
rejoice!

MAY 30

Be merciful, even as your Father is merciful.

Luke 6:36

❧❧

The trials of life can become tedious and the ravenous attacks by others, trying. It is easy to lose patience and to push back. Still, I call My children to forbearance. I ask them to extend mercy to those around them as I am extending it as well.

Mercy begins in the heart. Here, the humble recognize that they are made from dust with no particular merit of their own. These can see this same condition in their fellow man. Mercy is made alive by the awareness that an all-powerful God has bestowed His kindness upon all of mankind. Though undeserved, I have made mercy a factor in each person's life—whether they are a child of Mine or not. It is the very longsuffering of God and the natural result of unconditional love in action.

Let My loving mercy lead you each day. Allow it to mark each of your steps along the way. Pass it on freely to others. Celebrate as it spreads one heart at a time in the world.

MAY 31

You therefore must be perfect, as
your heavenly Father is perfect.

Matthew 5:48

❧

Perfection is completion. In Me, each of My children can be made complete. Apart from Me, completion is impossible for them.

It is not possible to walk in the world and endure its many challenges on your own. Why? Because I did not create you to be perfect. If you were, you would be independent of Me and could walk *apart* from Me—always doing the right thing, always having the right attitude, always free from self-seeking motives. Instead, I created you to walk *with* Me. And I told you that apart from Me, you could not do the works I give you to do. How then is it possible for you to be perfect in your dealings with others, as I have asked? There is only one way—by being completed by Me.

You are My precious child. Together, we can successfully walk through the kingdom. Do not grow weary in your walk. Perfection only comes one step at a time with Me at your side. Allow Me to make each thought, word, action, and attitude complete in My perfection.

JUNE

Battle lines are drawn. Jesus against Satan.
Angels against demons. The kingdom of God
against the kingdom of darkness. Truth against
deception. The battle rages all around, both
seen and unseen. Victory belongs to Jesus.

JUNE 1

*Then he will say to those on his left, 'Depart
from me, you cursed, into the eternal fire
prepared for the devil and his angels.'*

Matthew 25:41

༁

I have a great heavenly host who do My bidding. I send
them to protect My children and to fight on their behalf.
Likewise, Satan has his demonic multitude. Though not as
numerous, these are determined in their stance against Me
and all who are Mine.

A vast spiritual reality exists just beyond the visible
fabric of the universe. Spirit beings of tremendous power
are at war. It is pure good against polluted evil. Many do
not understand this unseen world. To them, it seems like
fantasy. Some dismiss it altogether. Others make idols of
these beings, both the evil and the good. I set My angels
among My children for protection, and each has their own
guard. These do My bidding in all things. By My command
they keep My precious ones from calamities large and
small. Likewise, Satan assigns demons to harass and
oppress My children. These evil ones are active in many
ways, none of which are good.

Be wise and understand the nature of the spirit world
around you. It is the power behind much of the physical
world. I am your strong tower. Stay close to Me. I will guide
you safely along the way.

June 2

What is your name?

Luke 8:30

୶୶

The spirit world around you is not a vague, cosmic occurrence. It is real, and it is specific. All who inhabit it have names—some given, some assumed. As with your name, these give identities to the individuals.

I created each of the angels. I gave every one of them a name. As with all names, each signified the dignity of its holder with an expression of My esteem for them. Then, the great rebellion came. Those who participated fell from their positions in My kingdom. They became hideous beings in their hatred for Me. These pridefully rejected the names I gave them and adopted those of their own design. They now lurk in the darkness as individuals and in groups, hatching vicious schemes against My beloved.

As you are loved by Me, you are hated by Satan and those he has assigned to destroy you. Walk with purpose, My child, and be aware of their scheming. Hold My hand. Let Me lead you to safe pastures.

JUNE 3

*You mute and deaf spirit, I command you, come
out of him and never enter him again.*

Mark 9:25

❧

Each demon is a specialist. Each has an assignment. These
are specific in nature and deadly in intent. Your downfall as
My follower is the goal, and obstructing your calling is the
objective.

I have given you a calling in this life so you can fulfill
your great purpose of bringing glory to our Father. This
calling is significant and important. By it, you walk into
your destiny and then are brought home to Me with great
joy. Many of My children do not understand My plans for
them. I tell you plainly, the demons do. These evil ones
work night and day to thwart My plans and lure the
unsuspecting from My path and into the wilderness. There,
far from Me, they work their deceit to bring My plans to
naught and My children to destruction. *Understand what
this means!*

My child, your calling is important to Me. Do not walk
through this life dazed and confused by the wiles of the
enemy. Instead, walk circumspectly with a singleness of
purpose—your calling. Shelter often in the shadow of My
wings. There, you are safe from the onslaught of the evil
ones.

JUNE 4

The thief comes only to steal and kill and destroy. I came that they may have life and have it abundantly.

John 10:10

❧❧

I am the giver of life. Abundance is found in Me. The evil ones are the carriers of death. They seek to strip each life bare.

In Me, you live and move and have your being. I take all you have to give, multiply it, and bring it forth in profusion. My living water flows through you like a spring in the desert. It brings refreshment to all who share in it. But thieves lurk in the shadows. They seek to lay waste to your life. They want to steal all that is good and make it barren. They want you dead. Destruction of your testimony is a high honor among them.

Stay on the path of life with Me. Do not tarry or turn to the left or the right. I am your only shield. Walk with Me so I can hedge you in and keep you out of the grasp of the destroyers.

JUNE 5

Heal the sick, raise the dead, cleanse
lepers, cast out demons.

Matthew 10:8

❧

My followers are My hands and feet in the world. I send them where I will. I do wondrous things through them. This is one of many ways I am at work in the world.

Many believe I have stopped working miracles through My children. They point to the musings of the church fathers from the past. They seek out Scripture verses to make their case. They search the world over with unseeing eyes and unbelieving hearts. I tell you, these will see only what their hearts desire to see. But those who walk with Me in faith will see great works performed through their hands. I will heal. I will cast out. I will raise the dead. As I work quietly in the world, these miracles will open the hearts of those who see them.

Doing My work through your hands is a great delight to Me. It is possible only because you walk closely with Me in great faith. Look around you with spiritual eyes. Listen for the command of My voice. Let us see what can be done in this unbelieving world.

JUNE 6

I saw Satan fall like lightning from heaven.

Luke 10:18

☙❧

Satan has been defeated. The sentence pronounced in the Garden of Eden has been carried out. He bruised Me. I crushed him. Now, he fights the desperate fight of the vanquished, seeking his final victims before the end. The battles rage, but the war is won.

With every act of obedience, My children hasten Satan's fall. I have been watching him tumble since I walked upon the earth as a man. Soon, he will be no more. He will find his place in the lake of fire with the rest of his rebellious demons. For now, though, he still roars as he walks upon the earth. In heaven, he continues his accusations against My beloved. Be watchful and wary as he falls. He is desperate to destroy because he knows his time to do so is short. He is vicious, and those with him are merciless.

You are a part of My great army on earth—My Church. Together, we tear at Satan's kingdom one act and word and thought at a time. I have won the victory, but you have many battles yet to fight. Take your place in the ranks. Listen to the voice of your Commander today.

June 7

Behold, I have given you authority to tread on serpents and scorpions, and over all the power of the enemy, and nothing shall hurt you.

Luke 10:19

❧

All authority in heaven and on earth belongs to Me. I give it freely to My disciples to use as I direct them. Those who are wise listen to My voice. Those who are foolish run off on their own.

When My children walk with Me, I am responsible for their protection. I am their great shield. Only what I allow passes through to them. These are the ones who rightly use My authority as I direct. Others of My children get out from behind My protection. These go off into the midst of battles of their choosing, proclaiming My name and carrying My banner. But I am not with them, and My authority is not found in their works. These do not understand that by their very actions they are exposed to the full fury of the enemy. They have no shield and are no match for their adversaries.

When we walk together, there is no occasion for fear. I give you My authority to do My works. I stand before you and behind you as your shield. Be fearless today in doing all I ask of you.

JUNE 8

*Nevertheless, do not rejoice in this, that the
spirits are subject to you, but rejoice that
your names are written in heaven.*

Luke 10:20

❦

Regardless of the task you are about for Me today, find your
true joy in belonging to Me. This keeps our walk fresh and
alive, giving no place to fear or weariness.

My true servants work humbly for the kingdom. They
know I give them the power they wield in this life. They
rejoice in being included in the great work I am doing upon
the earth. But some of My children have forgotten this vital
truth. They have been deceived in their pursuit of accolades
from the crowds. They do not find their joy in the kingdom
but in the fame and notoriety of the world. These are
mistaken. In their pride, they think more highly of
themselves than they should. Do not be like them. Instead,
seek My approval alone.

You are highly prized by Me because your name is
written in the Book of Life. It is My great pleasure to give
you works to do for My kingdom on earth. Walk humbly by
the power of the Holy Spirit working through you. Seek My
face above all else.

JUNE 9

*Every kingdom divided against itself is laid waste,
and no city or house divided against itself will
stand. And if Satan casts out Satan, he is divided
against himself. How then will his kingdom stand?*

Matthew 12:25-26

❧

In unity, My Church has tremendous power. In disarray, it is brought to nothing. This is a great truth for participating in My kingdom work.

Satan and his followers are bound together in their hatred against Me and all who are Mine. There is no lack of unity in their purposeful efforts. With My children, however, this is not so. They have allowed disagreements over doctrine, traditions, and practices to shatter their unity. They have splintered into factions more focused on protecting their small earthly kingdoms than following Me in truth in My kingdom. Their hatred towards one another has overshadowed their proclamations of devotion to Me. Disharmony and strife have displaced the unity of love I have commanded them to demonstrate to the world.

Do not fight the religious battles of men. Instead, celebrate a shared love for Me. By the power of this love, the world will be transformed one heart at a time for the glory of My kingdom.

JUNE 10

But if it is by the Spirit of God that I cast out demons,
then the kingdom of God has come upon you.

Matthew 12:28

❧❧

The kingdom of God is spreading across the earth. Heart upon heart responds to the call of the Holy Spirit. It is the very power of God at work. Evil cannot stand before it but must flee. Captives are set free and cry out with joy!

I have plainly told My children that apart from Me they can do nothing. Demons are not subject to the power of mere mortals. They do not flee before man's words spoken over them. It is My power alone that makes them take flight. Many go into this great spiritual battle unprepared. They are not filled with the Spirit of God but are full of themselves. Their sinful ways have left holes in their armor. They are sent fleeing before the enemy. This is not the case with those who are wise. They go forward by My command and in My power. The kingdom advances all around them.

Do not go into the battle in the nakedness of your sin! Repent and be filled by the Holy Spirit. Only by My power do the demons flee. Only by the Holy Spirit does the kingdom advance. Let it be so in your life today!

JUNE 11

*But no one can enter a strong man's house and
plunder his goods, unless he first binds the strong
man. Then indeed he may plunder his house.*

Mark 3:27

❧

I created mankind lower in power and capabilities than My
angels. This same truth applies to the rebellious ones who
are now ruled by Satan in the world of demons. All of them
are subject to Me, both the good and the bad.

There is talk among My children about the binding of
Satan and his demons. I tell you plainly, most speak from
their ignorance. My kingdom is just with rules of spiritual
engagement that cannot be violated. Demons gain rights
through the decisions of people. These rights come with
permissions to oppress and infest. Demons are not bound
by the words a human speaks over them. They are bound
by Me when their permissions are revoked, and they are left
with no legal standing to act upon.

I am your deliverer! It is by the power of My word that
your tormentors are contained or cast aside. I created you
to live free from the bondage of the evil ones. When I set
you free, you are free indeed!

JUNE 12

This kind cannot be driven out by anything but prayer.

Mark 9:29

෧෬ඏ

The wise prepare for the battle ahead. They put their affairs in order before Me. This gives Me the freedom to work on their behalf.

Many do not understand the nature of fasting and prayer. They believe these practices somehow imbue them with a special power of their own. This is not the case. I created mankind as vessels of service for My use. These vessels can easily become contaminated by sin and every kind of willfulness. Because of this, My power is hampered, and great spiritual undertakings are not possible. Prayer and fasting prepare the vessel for use by emptying it of all that interferes with My power. When the vessel is prepared for the work, I can then flow through it to do mighty things.

I long to use you in My kingdom. You must first be made ready. Empty yourself completely in repentance before Me. Turn from your unpleasing ways and be made clean. I will then do astonishing things through you, the likes of which you have never seen!

June 13

Go.

Matthew 8:32

৯৶৶

By My word, the heavens and the earth were made. By My word, you were brought forth. By My word, the powers of darkness must flee.

Man is flesh and blood. His strength is small. This is by My perfect plan. I made man to be a conduit of My power in this life. So it is with My children. By My design, they can do nothing of kingdom value on their own. I must flow through them. This way, the whole world can see that I am at work. I possess the infinite power of the Godhead in My hand. By My authority, this power is unleashed.

I come to your rescue. With one word, I overpower the enemies of your soul. I know your strength is small. I remember that you are but dust. *Sit quietly and contemplate this.*

JUNE 14

For the one who is not against us is for us.

Mark 9:40

❦

I am at work in many different ways in the world. Do not be surprised when you see them. This is the vast kaleidoscope of My love—always seeking, always calling, always wooing.

I am not the dull God many of My followers make Me out to be. Just look at the variegated majesty of My creation! I am not shy in My expressions of love. I move the same way in the world around you. I do not use a set human formula to accomplish My plan. Instead, I use all types of people in all kinds of ways. This is My Body at its best. But My Church has placed boundaries around Me and limits on how I am allowed to use My children. They have defined the times and places where I might move. In rules and regulations they have bound My people and shackled them to timeworn traditions that only constrict My options. This is not My way. Read My Word. You will see Me working mostly outside the comfort zones of the religious conformists. Let Me do what I do! Do not attempt to constrain the hand of God!

You are unique. You were born at the time and place of My choosing. I will use you in ways that are not the same as those of My other children. I will send you to places they do not go and have you do what they do not. *Will you allow Me to use you as I choose?*

JUNE 15

See, you are well! Sin no more, that
nothing worse may happen to you.

John 5:14

❧

The narrow path is difficult, but it is safe. I illuminate the
places where your feet step. My goodness and mercy follow
you from pasture to pasture.

All along the path we walk are doors of spiritual
consequence. Captivity and bondage lurk just beyond their
thresholds. Some are familiar. Some are new. All are
dangerous to My precious children. Many have been
delivered from the bondage of demons that once enslaved
them with sickness and addictions. These know the
dangers that lie in wait behind the doors. The wise among
them pass quickly by and are kept safe. The dull of heart
open the doors and enter. These are devoured, and their
last state is worse than their first.

You have been set free. Do not become entangled once
again in the cords of your sin where larger shackles of
bondage await. I am the way of freedom. Let us remain on
the path I have set before you.

JUNE 16

Get behind me, Satan! You are a hindrance to me.

Matthew 16:23

∽∾

There is nothing good in Satan. Though he was created as My most beautiful angel and stood before the very throne of God, it was not enough for him. His rebellion was complete and is at work even to this day. His every thought is to hinder Me and the work I am doing upon the earth.

Most people are unaware that they are held under Satan's influence. They go about their business each day with little thought of why they are doing what they do. His orders are carried out by ranks of demons as they influence the many peoples of the earth with their evil whisperings to the human heart. My own children do not recognize the extent of this influence in their lives. They forget that everything they think, say, or do is either for My kingdom or for his.

You belong to Me. You are enlivened by the power of the Holy Spirit working within you. Do not become dull of heart. Be aware of what you think, what you say, and what you do. Turn from everything that hinders the advancement of My kingdom in your heart, in your life, and in the world.

JUNE 17

For you are not setting your mind on the
things of God, but on the things of man.

Matthew 16:23

❧

I give My very mind to My children. It is part of their new nature. As each comes to know Me better, they gain My perspective and way of thinking. Through tests and trials they are made wise.

When this happens or that occurs in someone's life, it draws a response from them. To many, the first reaction comes from the limited perspective of the human heart. Their eyes cannot see nor their minds comprehend what I am doing. Even those who walk closely with Me struggle at times to understand how I am at work in the situations of their lives. Man's way is not My way. Man's thoughts are not Mine. I see all that is possible, and I am working accordingly in the world as I implement My Father's plan. This is why I do what I do in the way I do it. Those who stop and sit before Me gain My perspective. The rest are left to wonder.

Put on My mind. Come close and think My thoughts. You will see a reason for the mosaic of circumstances in your life. I prepare your way with purpose. Walk with Me and discover what I am doing in your life.

JUNE 18

*Simon, Simon, behold, Satan demanded to
have you, that he might sift you like wheat.*

Luke 22:31

❧

I am the Lord of all. Satan and his demons are subject to
Me. I have defeated them. Permissions determine their
rights and the extent of their access to My people.

Satan is your accuser. He brings indictment after
indictment before Me day and night. He asks for permission
to send his demons to attack you. It is only by My
authorization that this access is granted. When I do allow
it, My objective is to do a great work in your heart,
separating the wheat from the chaff or the metal from the
dross in your life. In this way, My children can be made
pure in heart and prepared for the rest of our journey
together.

You are made righteous by My blood. Even so, I allow
you to be sifted from time to time according to those areas
in your life that are not yet pleasing to Me. Cooperate with
Me to eliminate these things before I grant greater access to
your enemy. Whoever falls on Me will be broken but not
crushed. *Do you hear the words I am speaking to you?*

JUNE 19

*Why are you sleeping? Rise and pray that
you may not enter into temptation.*

Luke 22:46

❧

My children are exposed to many dangers in the world.
They take specific steps to protect themselves from physical
danger each day. *But what of the spiritual threats?*

The enemy wants to destroy My people. Temptations are
their favored method of attack. While temptations live in the
fleshly realms of the world, they are spiritual in nature.
Each temptation calls for a decision to be made between
following Me or following Satan. Their subtlety is only
equaled by the craftiness behind the trap being laid. The
objective is the ruination of a testimony, either through
slow erosion or catastrophic collapse. Those who are asleep
to this danger will readily fall. Those who are aware of the
weakness of their flesh cry out to Me for protection from
themselves.

Do not sleep and do not slumber. Your adversary seeks
you as a lion stalks his prey. In humbleness be aware of
your propensity for self-exaltation and self-satisfaction. Ask
Me to work in your heart so you may not go the way of a
brute beast to the slaughter. Ask to always see a clear way
of escape.

JUNE 20

*It is written, 'Man shall not live by bread alone, but
by every word that comes from the mouth of God.'*

Matthew 4:4

❧❧

When temptations come upon you, remember the
steadfastness of My truths. Upon these, you have sure
footing to parry the lying thrusts of the evil ones.

Every temptation is based on a lie. These challenge the
preferences of your heart by appealing to the hungers of
your flesh. Each temptation is shrouded in the half-truth of
deception, allowing you to see what you want to see. Miry
clay surrounds the offer, making the footing more
treacherous with every step you take toward it. My truth is
your only defense. By it, your preference for Me is made
clear. Through it, you can see the lie for what it is. With it,
you remain on solid ground.

Hide My truth in your heart. Let it sharpen your spirit as
a honing stone does iron. Allow it to infuse all of your ways.
In the day of your temptation, it will show you the way of
escape. This you can be sure of.

June 21

*Again it is written, 'You shall not put
the Lord your God to the test.'*

Matthew 4:7

❧

I am true and My way is sure. I measure each of your steps.
Will I find them true or false?

Some of My children make it a habit to run toward evil.
These say to themselves that they only want the thrill of the
possibility but not the reality of partaking. They are like
moths attracted to the flame, never considering the
consuming heat before them. Around and around they fly,
ever closer, ever hotter. In the end, they are devoured by
evil due to the proudness of their hearts. So it is with all
who test My patience toward them.

Take the route of escape from evil when it is offered to
you. Do not think you can elude capture by doubling back
time after time. You will pass a point where escape is
impossible. There, you will fall by the base desires of your
fleshly heart. Many have tested Me in this and have joined
the ranks of the fallen. I do not wish the same for you. Let
Me light your path and make your step sure.

JUNE 22

*Be gone, Satan! For it is written, 'You shall worship
the Lord your God and him only shall you serve.'*

Matthew 4:10

৵৵৻

My children were created to worship and serve the Father
through Me. Bringing Him glory is the great purpose that is
to drive their lives. When this is their focus, darkness flees.

Satan and his demons seek to divert the attention of My
children from what is eternal to what is temporal. They do
this by crafty appeals to the lust of the eyes and flesh where
mankind is most easily led astray by pride. They know it is
not possible to serve two masters, and they intend to be the
ones served. They seek to exploit the human tendency to
look inward, keeping My children from looking upward to
the one true God.

You were made to love Me. It is the only possible
fulfillment of your heart's desires. Run to the light where
there is no darkness. You will find Me there.

JUNE 23

When I was with you day after day in the
temple, you did not lay hands on me. But this
is your hour, and the power of darkness.

Luke 22:53

☙❧

The world moves steadily forward on the Father's timetable
and according to His plan. Times and seasons come and go,
bringing both darkness and light upon the sons and
daughters of men. So it will be until the end.

There are places of light where I move freely and areas of
darkness where I am hindered. There are times of
awakening where people are quickened by the Holy Spirit
and times of slumber where evil settles upon the land like
locusts. Even so, the Holy Spirit moves as He wills, calling
those who will be Mine at their appointed times and places.
I hear the moans of My children when they traverse the
dark and their cries of joy when they dance in the light. I
work all things to their ultimate good so My Father's plan is
executed according to His will. This is the great mystery of
His sovereignty working in step with the individual wills of
mankind.

You will experience times of darkness where evil has its
hour and times of light where evil is kept at bay. You do not
know these times—they can change in the blink of an eye.
Walk steadfastly with Me through them. Never let go of My
hand. Together, we will fulfill our Father's plans.

JUNE 24

Go your way; behold, I am sending you
out as lambs in the midst of wolves.

Luke 10:3

❧

Those who follow Me must depend on Me. Their resources are not enough for the work ahead.

Natural talents and aptitudes given at conception and honed by use can only take My children so far. Those who rely on these for My great work fall short of what I have planned. These have forgotten how the work of the kingdom is spiritual in nature and must be conducted by My power. I equip each of My followers supernaturally by the Holy Spirit and train them individually through unique life experiences. Even so, they are as lambs in the midst of wolves. If they do not stay close to Me, their Shepherd, they will be devoured.

Do not rely on the power of your flesh. It will fail you in the crucial moment. Instead, take all I have given you and go forth in faith down the path I open before you. Rely on Me to make the way clear through the many wolf packs we encounter along the way.

JUNE 25

Beware of false prophets, who come to you in sheep's clothing but inwardly are ravenous wolves.

Matthew 7:15

❧

What is false can be dressed to look like truth. Many times, it is only a matter of degrees. But underneath the familiar, deception lurks. The wool looks white, but the breath is that of a wolf.

The vain philosophies of the world try to crowd in. They take many in My Church captive. Lies are salted with enough truth to lead the unsuspecting away in error. Soon, what seems right to man supersedes My clear teachings. The firm foundation of truth is traded for shifting sands of opinion. Freedom to move as I direct is replaced by the bondage of groupthink and the expectation of conformity to man's standards. The flesh is fed while the spirit is starved. The sheep become infected by the disease of the wolves and wander away from their Shepherd.

Walk by the Holy Spirit and live by His discernment. Look with spiritual eyes and hear with spiritual ears. You will know My truth when you hear it. Listen for the sound of My voice calling to you in the midst of the tumult. Remain with Me in the pasture I have prepared for you.

JUNE 26

For false christs and false prophets will arise
and perform great signs and wonders, so as
to lead astray, if possible, even the elect.

Matthew 24:24

જ્જી

The world is being prepared for the great deception.
Already, those who are false are making their plans. Behind
them are the power of Satan and the spirit of antichrist.

My Church has been infiltrated by false prophets. These
speak pompously for Me, but My truth is not in them. Many
of My people willingly follow along. They delight in having
their ears tickled and their flesh entertained. They seek
experiences instead of the one true God. They strive for and
covet the riches of the world. They are empty cisterns ready
to be filled by the evil ones. I tell you truly, these will be fed
with what they seek *to the full.*

Do not be deceived! If you sow to the flesh, you will reap
of its weakness. Instead, strengthen your spirit in Me.
Then, the wolves will not take you in. You will stand!

JUNE 27

You will recognize them by their fruits.

Matthew 7:16

࿇

Wheat and grassy weeds can look much the same. I allow them to grow side by side until the final harvest. I then sort them according to the type of fruit they produced—righteousness or wickedness.

Many of My children are unaware that wolves are growing among them. They look around and all they see are sheep. The wolves have hidden themselves in a cloak of deceit. They dress like sheep would expect them to be dressed. They speak the same language. Even their behavior seems familiar enough so no alarm is raised. But here and there, the twisting of a truth, the excusing of a sin, or the espousing of a worldly philosophy betrays their identity to those who are keen in spirit. Those with spiritual eyes can see the fruits of their duplicitous ways.

I see the poisonous fruit of the weeds that grow in your midst. Do not become entangled with these weeds or allow them to siphon off My life-giving water. I will separate them at harvest time and throw them into the fire.

June 28

Whoever is not with me is against me, and whoever does not gather with me scatters.

Matthew 12:30

❧

There are only two sides in the great spiritual war. Each person is either with Me or against Me. Each is either helping to bring in the kingdom harvest or hindering the work. True neutrality is not possible.

The world stands against Me, its hatred on display for all to see. But not all of its people will admit to this. Some try to remain neutral, neither accepting Me fully nor condemning Me completely. But because they are not with Me, I see them as against Me. My followers are not strangers to the same lack of commitment. Many stand aloof from what I have clearly asked of them as one of My own. These have divided hearts that try to love both their self-centered ways and Me. I tell you, these very same ones get in the way of what I am trying to do and hinder the work of the kingdom. They confuse those who watch from the world and cause the weak within My Church to stumble.

I long for your heart to be fully Mine! I invite you to partake in My harvest. Encourage those around you in the work, and do not cause the weak to stumble. *Sit before Me and let us consider your walk to see if you are gathering with Me or scattering.*

JUNE 29

You are of your father the devil, and your will is to do your father's desires. He was a murderer from the beginning, and does not stand in the truth, because there is no truth in him. When he lies, he speaks out of his own character, for he is a liar and the father of lies.

John 8:44

చొన్

My children walk with Me and do My will. Satan's children walk with him and do his will. My children become more like Me. His become more like him. This is how it has always been and how it will be until the end. *Let those who have ears hear what I am saying.*

My Church spends too much energy complaining about the world. I did not call My children to complain but to spread My love and share My mercy. Why would you expect the world to be any different than it is? Why would you expect slaves of sin to stop sinning? Why would you expect those who stand against Me to be for you? Let us get back to the work I have called you to do and leave the complaining behind.

You are a pilgrim in this world. You do not belong here. This place is not your home. Rejoice in this! Be about the work I have given you to do. Spread My love with joy and My mercy with kindness. Expect nothing in return.

JUNE 30

My sheep hear my voice, and I know
them, and they follow me.

John 10:27

❧

I love My children! I know they are like sheep and in need of a shepherd. I am their Shepherd. I call out to them and they run to Me. The goats do not listen. They follow the voice of another—the thief who comes to steal, kill, and destroy.

My sheep know I love them. They love Me in return. They go about listening for My voice. When they hear it, they run to Me and seek to follow where I lead. My sheep learn to stay with Me. They go with Me to My pastures and do not wander off in search of their own. My sheep seek My approval alone, counting the approval of other sheep or shepherds as nothing to be desired. They find great comfort in belonging to Me and are satisfied with My ways.

You have answered My call and belong to Me. I wash you in My love. I carry you in My arms. I protect you with My staff. I feed you in My fields. You follow Me along the narrow way, walking in My footsteps. I shout in delight that you are Mine!

JULY

Jesus calls out to us, 'Follow Me.' This is an invitation to join Him in the great work of building His kingdom. It is a privilege of great consequence where we exchange the life we had planned for the life He has for us.

July 1

Follow me.

Matthew 9:9

❧

I extend this invitation to all whom the Father has chosen for the kingdom. It is a call of privilege. It is a call to become the very children of God. It is a call to the life I have chosen for you.

Many do not understand the weightiness of the words *Follow Me*. They think in terms of avoiding hell or becoming part of a local church. Some act as if they were joining a club and these words were merely an invitation for membership. I tell you plainly, all who think such thoughts are deceived. Instead, these words are a call to join Me in the great work of My kingdom. They are an invitation to become a son or daughter of God. They are a summons to exchange all of your plans for all of My plans.

I have called you to join Me in a great adventure. It is not merely an invitation to a one-time decision. It is a summons to a new way of life. It is a call to leave and to cleave—to separate from your old ways and to firmly grasp My new ways. *Is this what you have done?*

JULY 2

For which of you, desiring to build a tower, does not first sit down and count the cost, whether he has enough to complete it? Otherwise, when he has laid a foundation and is not able to finish, all who see it begin to mock him, saying, 'This man began to build and was not able to finish.'

Luke 14:28-30

❧

My salvation is a free gift. You do not deserve it, and you cannot earn it by works. I have paid the price in full. Even so, following Me comes with a cost to you, and that cost is the surrendering of your will to Me.

A true decision to follow Me requires that a choice be made about who will rule your life. Many have been deceived. They have not been told about this cost. They made decisions based on emotion or motive. They asked Me to save them without committing to My lordship in their lives. This is why I have told you clearly the cost of following Me. Each person should carefully consider this cost to the best of their ability, making sure they are willing to pay the price.

I want you to finish well. I have set a path before you. I long to share the journey with you each day. *Are you willing to lay aside your will and follow Mine?*

JULY 3

*If anyone would come after me, let him deny himself
and take up his cross daily and follow me.*

Luke 9:23

ॐ

A cross is an instrument of death. Those who carry one
signify their allegiance to Me and My purposes for their
lives. These demonstrate to the world that they are daily
walking with Me by dying to themselves, the same as I did
for them.

Many have made light of taking up one's cross. They talk
flippantly about their problems as being 'the cross they
have to bear'. This is not what taking up the cross means. I
died upon a cross so others could come to Me and walk
with Me into eternity. I call all who would do so to daily die
more to themselves so they can daily live more in Me. This
dying requires denying. It demands the bending of the will
until it conforms to Mine. The cross is a reminder of two
deaths—yours and Mine.

My child, I know how difficult it is for you to willfully pick
up your cross each day. I understand how tenaciously the
flesh clings to life. I will help you crucify your flesh one day
at a time. As you do, I will become more alive in you. This is
My promise to you.

JULY 4

For whoever would save his life will lose it, but
whoever loses his life for my sake will save it.
For what does it profit a man if he gains the
whole world and loses or forfeits himself?

Luke 9:24-25

❧❧

Following Me is the process of losing one's life. It begins with a commitment to Me. Then, there is the daily follow-through on this commitment. With each step down the path, less of you and more of Me is found.

Many are not willing to make the initial commitment. These want My offer of eternal life but will not give Me their lives for My use. Instead, they want to save their lives for themselves and live them as they see fit. Because these only pay lip service to My offer, it is to them I will say on the last day, 'Depart, I never knew you.' Others commit to giving Me their lives but do not follow through on their pledge of fidelity. After the initial excitement of salvation wears thin, these fight Me day after day and will not walk with Me. They spend their lives wrestling with Me instead of losing their lives for My sake. Listen as I tell you, these will get to heaven but without rewards.

I have laid My life down for you. I have bought you with a great price. You belong to Me. Rejoice that this is so! I ask you to lay your life at My feet one day at a time and refrain from taking it back up again. This will be to your eternal profit in heaven.

July 5

No one who puts his hand to the plow and
looks back is fit for the kingdom of God.

Luke 9:62

❧

I hold the futures of all who follow Me. I have plans for their lives. Those who walk with Me share My aspirations. They know there is no better way for them on earth. *Have you taken this to heart?*

I invite My followers to share in the great enterprise of building My Church on earth. The work I have for each of them is specific. As a group, the effort becomes the comprehensive fulfillment of the Father's plan. Many want to be a part of what I am doing. Some, though, are not fit for the work. These do not keep their eyes on Me. The furrows they plow are crooked and ineffective, marked with the telltale signs of stopping and starting over and over again. They keep looking back with longing eyes at the world behind them. They regret having started a work that does not truly hold their heart captive. Many stop completely, turning from all I have for them and running back to their old lives.

I have called you out of the world. I have put you to work in the kingdom. Remain steadfast with Me. Let your furrows on the face of the earth be straight, deep, and of much consequence. Such are My aspirations for you!

JULY 6

*So therefore, any one of you who does not
renounce all that he has cannot be my disciple.*

Luke 14:33

෨∾෨

Friendship with the world places a person in direct
opposition to Me. Any plans that are not Mine oppose My
work. Those who practice such things can never become My
disciples. Their lives will stand as testimonies to this truth.

My last command was that My children would make
disciples of others. This is the great march of My kingdom
through the world. But how is this possible if My children
are not first disciples themselves? Discipleship is learned.
There are no shortcuts. It begins by taking one's eyes off of
the things of the world so the heart can focus on Me. Those
who do this learn My ways and become My disciples. It is a
great indictment against My Church that most are not My
disciples. The majority of My people do not follow where I
lead or do what I ask. Their relationship with Me is one of
convenience. They have little desire in learning My ways.
Their hearts are held captive by worldly pursuits.

Transforming you into My disciple is a great pleasure for
Me. As we walk together each day, I will teach you My ways.
As we discuss things great and small, you will come to
know My heart. As you see situations come and go, you will
take on the perspective of My thoughts. My goal is for you
to become like Me. This is the true meaning of discipleship.

JULY 7

Repent, for the kingdom of heaven is at hand.

Matthew 4:17

☙❧

Following Me requires that you cease following other things. Becoming My disciple means you are learning My ways and forsaking the ways of the world. Both of these demand that you turn from every way to My way. This is not possible until your heart surrenders to Me.

The ways of repentance have largely been lost to My Church. They have been replaced with blame shifting and esteem building. Repentance does not look for excuses. It does not seek affirmation. Repentance is based on brokenness and the humility of owned outcomes. It is more than being sorry. It is a change of the mind, which is a change of the heart. Emotional appeals cannot change a heart. Only I can. So I require anyone who would repent to cry out to Me so I can change their heart. The evidence of a changed heart is found in the action of changed ways. Changed ways lead to changed lives, and these are a characteristic of My kingdom.

I love you too much to let you go astray. The Holy Spirit convicts you, and My love brings you to repentance. This is the way of all My disciples. It is the way of the kingdom of heaven.

JULY 8

And the one who falls on this stone will be broken to pieces;
and when it falls on anyone, it will crush him.

Matthew 21:44

ॐ∻☙

I am the Chief Cornerstone. Upon Me, the kingdom of
heaven is built with truth and justice, love and mercy.
Whoever falls on Me will be broken in love and mercy.
Whoever I fall on will be crushed by truth and justice.

It is with tender love and patient mercy that I receive all
who throw themselves upon Me with humble and contrite
hearts. I will not cast them aside but will hug them to
Myself and restore them to My fellowship. This is My heart's
desire. Those who stand aloof in the hardness of a proud
heart are not granted such tenderness. Instead, I will crush
them in the midst of their rebellious ways. These will feel
the sting of My justice and the searing heat of My truth.

I have called you to be Mine. Run to Me and throw
yourself upon My love and mercy. I will pick you up and
hold you close. I will brush you off and set you once again
on your path. We will walk in the joy of restored fellowship.

JULY 9

For many are called, but few are chosen.

Matthew 22:14

᠅

I call out through the Holy Spirit to all who the Father has named. I patiently work in their lives to bring them to Myself. Those who respond are given to Me by My Father. These are the chosen ones.

Those who are called hear My voice and know I am calling to them. This is by the working of the Holy Spirit who makes Me known in the world. These called ones must decide if they will respond and come to Me. It is true that many are called. It is even a greater truth that few respond and are chosen to be Mine. Many believe My call goes out to all of mankind, but this is not the case. These labor in vain as they try to bring everyone into the kingdom. But only those who are called can respond. And those who answer the call are fewer in number than what is popular to believe. The wise will understand what this means and go only to those to whom they are sent.

You have been chosen because you answered My call. It is a great and wondrous thing. Rejoice that your name is written in My book! All of heaven has celebrated!

JULY 10

*Come to me, all who labor and are heavy
laden, and I will give you rest.*

Matthew 11:28

৵৵

I offer abundant life to My children. This is not the
abundance of earthly things, as many believe. It is a life
filled with My fellowship—Me abiding in you.

Many labor day upon day under the yoke of religion.
These carry burdens of traditions and practices. They are
weighed down by the requirements of rules and regulations.
Shackles of conformity and expectation keep them from
dancing in delight before Me. Rest is nowhere to be found in
all of their *doing*. I offer all who come to Me a better way.
Rules are replaced by love. Condemnation is eradicated by
mercy. Works are exchanged for grace. Truth overcomes the
error of traditions and practices. Freedom supersedes
conformity. Rest is found in a close relationship with Me.

There is no earning My love. Works cannot buy My
acceptance. You are Mine. My abundant nature is yours for
all of eternity. Come and rest in My love. Let My arms of
mercy and grace hold you. I will never leave you or forsake
you. Enter into My rest!

JULY 11

*Take my yoke upon you, and learn from me, for I am
gentle and lowly in heart, and you will find rest for your
souls. For my yoke is easy, and my burden is light.*

Matthew 11:29-30

৵৵

My yoke is easy because I do most of the work. My burden
is light because I carry most of the load. I am not a God
who is far off and out of your reach. I am One who walks by
your side.

The wise among My children eagerly accept My yoke. It is
not a single yoke where they must pull the load but a
double yoke where I pull in tandem with them. By this
yoke, My followers learn from Me as we walk together on
the journey. They discover how to go where I go and keep
pace with all I am doing. Because I am gentle and meek, I
take most of the burden upon Myself. My children benefit
continuously by the power of My strength. For the stiff-
necked, however, this is not so. I allow them to feel the full
burden of the load in their rebellion. These find themselves
exhausted as they pull against Me and try to do things their
way. *Reflect on this great truth.*

Learn from Me. I know the way and how to get there.
Walk side by side with Me. Accept My strength as yours. Let
gentleness and meekness be your hallmark as we travel.

July 12

Do not be afraid; from now on you will be catching men.

Luke 5:10

❧❧

I call My children to tremendous undertakings. I show them My power in the midst of our work together. By this, they can know that all I have asked of them is possible through Me.

Whatever I call My followers to do is possible. The difference between *futility* and *result* in the effort is My miraculous power. Some make it a practice to try to do the work of the kingdom in their own strength. These may find some worldly success, but it is never as I planned it to be. As Peter found out, I am the One who steers the fish toward the boat. As My children discover, I am the One who makes their efforts consequential. I fill their nets where others have come up empty. Impossible tasks can be approached with confidence because I am at work. And this makes all of the difference.

Do not be dismayed at what I have asked you to do. I know you are not up to the task on your own. Do not fear. I will supply the miracles and move the hearts so the work is done. I look only for your willingness and faith. These mix well with My power to create results.

JULY 13

A disciple is not above his teacher, but everyone
when he is fully trained will be like his teacher.

Luke 6:40

৵৽

I am the embodiment of wisdom. I give this wisdom to those of Mine who seek it. As we converse along the way, I teach them My ways and impart to them My perspectives. Each day, they become more like Me.

Many of My children place little value on becoming My disciples. Instead, they want fame and notoriety, riches and possessions, and even lives of ease without suffering. These very same desires among the religious elite 2,000 years ago brought My ire down upon them. I challenged their self-serving ambitions then and extended the same invitation as I do today: *Follow Me.* Worldly expectations within My Church capture the attention of My people, keeping them from becoming more like Me. No one can truly follow Me with a divided heart. And that is all I ask...*Follow Me.*

The greatest compliment you can give to Me is to become like Me. This is so because you cannot become like Me without the desire, the effort, and the perseverance to walk with Me through all that your life brings to you. I desire to spend much time with you so this can be accomplished. *Do you share in My desire?*

JULY 14

Foxes have holes, and birds of the air have nests,
but the Son of Man has nowhere to lay his head.

Luke 9:58

೭ംക

Following Me is not always easy or convenient. It requires a willingness to leave the familiar and comfortable behind while relying completely on Me for everything.

When I walked upon the earth with My first disciples, we journeyed as My Father led. We depended on His provision as we travelled. It is the same with My disciples today. I ask them to step out in faith and do the works I give them to do. Many times, they cannot see how it is possible—there is not enough money or food, there is no obvious place for them to stay, or the necessary doors seem closed to them. But it is here that I provide for them as they continue to follow Me.

As you walk with Me, I grow your faith by providing what you need when you need it. I ask you to step out of your comfort zone and into the unknown. Always be looking for what I am doing. Always be ready to accept My provision, even from unexpected sources. Know I am at work on your behalf.

JULY 15

If anyone would be first, he must
be last of all and servant of all.

Mark 9:35

❧

My eyes search the world over for those of My children who
have given themselves fully to Me. These I lift up in their
humbleness. I do great things through them.

The human heart seeks to be exalted. Many of My
children have fallen prey to this base desire. These seek the
approval of those around them. They want to be admired
for their positions, possessions, or personalities. They serve
others with motives. As these children increase within
themselves, I decrease. This is not My way. Mine is the path
of humbleness. I raise up the lowly to do My great work. I
use those others would call foolish in their devotion to Me.
These have decreased so I can increase in them. I consider
them My special ones because I own their hearts.

I want to be able to use you profitably for My work. I ask
that you not be quick to seek the recognition of others, but
seek only My approval. You are precious to Me. I want to
number you with My special ones. I want to own your
humble heart. *Will you allow this to be so?*

JULY 16

You lack one thing: go, sell all that you have
and give to the poor, and you will have
treasure in heaven; and come, follow me.

Mark 10:21

৵৵

I know what holds each of My children back from fully
giving themselves to Me. I see these things deep within their
hearts. I ask that each of these hindrances be willingly laid
at My feet.

The human heart is filled with preferences. These drive
attitudes and behaviors. Many times, My children are not
aware of these biases and desires that lurk deep within.
Yet, I see them, and I know they will hinder our walk
together. I put My finger on each of these areas in My
timing. I draw them to the surface and make them known. I
ask My children to deal with these dark spots of the heart
and to turn away from them in repentance. I remove their
burdens one by one and lead them to walk in true freedom
in Me.

I correct those I love. I point out areas that need to
change so you can walk ever more freely in Me. Each time
you surrender an area to Me, you will experience lightness
in your soul and purity in your heart. I am then able to use
you more effectively for the kingdom. *Stop and listen for the*
area I am asking of you right now.

JULY 17

For I have come to set a man against his father, and
a daughter against her mother, and a daughter-in-
law against her mother-in-law. And a person's
enemies will be those of his own household.

Matthew 10:35-36

୬୦୧

I did not come to bring peace upon the earth as many
believe. Instead, I came to be the tipping point for all of
humanity. No one can remain neutral where I am involved.

I call out to all the Father has named. Others do not hear
My voice. In this way, all of humanity is divided as if by a
sword. Those who respond are brought out of darkness and
into My light. They come into conflict with all who remain in
darkness because darkness and light do not mix. Even
within the love bonds of a family this happens. The one who
has responded to My call now has a different nature from
the others. The common ground of the family relationship is
superseded by a far greater relationship with Me. This is a
painful consequence of sin entering the world when Adam
fell. I give extra strength to those I call to walk this path so
they can remain steadfast and sure.

You were called out of darkness and into My light. You
have left everything to follow Me. You have enemies now,
but you also have the greatest friend of all—Me. You have
left family and friends, but you have gained a new family
and new friends—My Church.

JULY 18

*Whoever loves father or mother more than me is
not worthy of me, and whoever loves son or
daughter more than me is not worthy of me.*

Matthew 10:37

&

When I call My followers out, I call them as individuals. I
deal with them personally, directing their specific paths. I
ask them to put our relationship first in all things—above
all people, all possessions, all plans, and all desires. This is
the walk of My disciples.

Many attempt to follow Me while following others. They
gather input from people of influence in their lives. They
make decisions and *then* ask Me to bless them. This is not
following Me. It is the way of a divided heart. Those who
truly love Me keep our relationship as the priority. Though
they may seek counsel from others, they lay the final
decisions before Me and wait for My direction. These do not
seek My stamp of approval on what has already been
decided. Instead, they seek Me, knowing I will bless what I
have directed.

I called you out from among the many. You stand before
Me as an individual, not as a family or church member. I
seek to direct your path. I want to be your focus. Do not go
with the crowd. Go with Me. Do not give your heart to
another. Let Me hold it in My hands and direct it as I will.

JULY 19

And what I say to you I say to all: Stay awake.

Mark 13:37

❧

I do not know the time of My return. Only My Father knows. I stand ready for His call. Likewise, you do not know the day or time when I will ask something of you. Watch and wait so you are ready.

Many of My children have been lulled to sleep. They have fallen in step with the rhythms of this busy world. Their hearts have become dull. They do not listen for the sound of My voice, and when I speak, they cannot discern it from the other voices that cry out to them day and night. Those who will walk with Me must know the sound of My voice. They need to listen intently for My commands. They should always be ready to stop what they are doing in order to go in a new direction. Such listening and obeying is the mark of My disciples. I teach them to do this as we walk along the way.

Keep your heart sharp and do not slumber. I have much for you to do and specific times when these things are to be done. I will not always come to you when you expect, so stay awake with a watchful heart—ever alert, ever ready. *When I speak to you, can you hear My voice?*

JULY 20

I do not say to you seven times, but seventy-seven times.

Matthew 18:22

৵৽

Forgiveness goes hand in hand with love and mercy. It is an act of the will, not of the emotions. All who walk with Me are quick to forgive. These do not wish to drink from the bitter cup of revenge. They seek out the forgiveness of others so peace may abound.

People are imperfect. They can and will offend and hurt—some only once and others many times over. This is why I call My children to forgive others or to seek forgiveness from those they have offended. This is the way of love and mercy that marks My disciples out from all others. My children tend to forget the many things I have forgiven them of in the past or am forgiving them of even now. It is good to reflect on these when an offense comes from another.

Just as unforgiveness is a corrosive poison in the soul, forgiveness is a healing balm. As I have forgiven you, forgive others. As I have extended My hand of love and mercy to you, extend the same to others. *Is there someone you should forgive right now? Is there a wrong for which you should seek forgiveness today?*

JULY 21

*You know that those who are considered rulers of the
Gentiles lord it over them, and their great ones exercise
authority over them. But it shall not be so among you. But
whoever would be great among you must be your servant,
and whoever would be first among you must be slave of all.*

Mark 10:42-44

৵৽৻৶

I am the Lord of all. Yet, I came to earth as a servant. I am
the King of all. Yet, I washed the dirty feet of My first
disciples. Even though I hold the entire universe together in
My hand, I still make time for all of My children.

The fleshly heart of man seeks to control and rule over
others. Those who walk with Me are not immune to this
tendency. Some seek elevation above others like a king over
his subjects. These enjoy the service of many on their
behalf. They believe this is how it should be after the
initiative they have taken, the sacrifices they have made, or
the years they have served. They justify such behavior out
of a sense of entitlement. But this is the world's thinking
and not My way. I call My disciples to serve others as I have
done and continue to do. None of My children are above
their Master.

I have called you to be the servant of all. I do this so I
can be the One to raise you up. Give of your heart, your
hands, and your time to others. Do not think more highly of
yourself than you should or consider yourself to be more
worthy than others working with you for the kingdom. I love
you. That is enough.

JULY 22

*Therefore render to Caesar the things that are Caesar's,
and to God the things that are God's.*

Matthew 22:21

༒

The kingdoms of the world are not My kingdoms. I set up kings and nations and tear them down according to My Father's plans.

My kingdom is not of this world. Many of My children have forgotten this. They try with all of their might to bring nations and rulers under their control but to no avail. They search for evidence that I am for one country and against another, but I do not take sides. My only concern with nations and rulers is the working out of My Father's plans on earth. I allow some to flourish for a time and a season, while others are held in check. Wherever I place My children, I expect them to give what they *must* to their rulers while giving what they *should* to Me. In this way, they can concentrate on becoming more like Me and spreading My love instead of on harnessing their governments and spreading their agendas. My kingdom will not be brought closer to completion by any governing class. It is only by the Holy Spirit working through My children one heart at a time that it will grow.

I have brought you forth and placed you upon the earth for this exact time in history. I have called you to Myself, and you have responded. Let us make building My kingdom the priority rather than building some kingdom of man. My Father's plan for the world will not be thwarted.

JULY 23

*You shall love the Lord your God with all your heart
and with all your soul and with all your mind. This
is the great and first commandment.*

Matthew 22:37-38

❦

This command is to be the first priority of all of My
children. From it flows all that is good in our walk upon the
earth.

Loving God with their entire being is not the priority of
most of My children. Many will say it is, but few have the
evidence to support their case. Instead, they have allowed
their circumstances to dictate their daily priorities.
Spouses, children, pets, jobs, wealth, possessions, status,
fame, food, experiences, and leisure all compete for the top
spot in the hearts of My followers. Loving God has become a
vague 'given' in their lives, with most believing that they do.
I tell you, this is not the case. If it were, many things would
be different with My people, and My Church would be
seeing My power flow like never before.

Give yourself completely over to loving the God who
made you and sustains you. Let your heart, mind, will, and
emotions sing out their love for Him. Let your attitudes and
actions give evidence of this fidelity. The world will be
amazed.

July 24

*And a second is like it: You shall
love your neighbor as yourself.*

Matthew 22:39

❧◦❧

This command is to be the second priority of all My
children. It is not possible if the first commandment is not
being followed, for out of the first, the second flows.

You can only love yourself once you understand how I
love you. Otherwise, you will love yourself from vanity or
loathe yourself from misunderstanding. Many of My
children are caught in these traps because they do not
know how I love them unconditionally. Likewise, you can
only love your neighbor if you understand how to love your
God. Otherwise, your love for others will fall short of what it
should be, becoming bogged down in motives, convenience,
and shallowness. This is why so few of My children express
unconditional love to their neighbors in the world—they
have not first learned how to love Me fully.

I love you. It is the complete love of accepting your
current state without conditions. I look to see if you will
take My love and express it to those around you. I shout
with gladness when you do! It means you love Me and have
accepted My love for you.

JULY 25

*And the King will answer them, 'Truly, I say
to you, as you did it to one of the least of
these my brothers, you did it to me.'*

Matthew 25:40

৵৽

The Holy Spirit has placed each of My children into the great body of believers, which is My Church. These are brothers and sisters by adoption into My family. Anyone who is not in My family is not a brother or sister.

Many in My Church do not understand this simple truth. They have wrongly taken on the burden of caring for the entire world and the related pressure of touching each person equally. They race around doing good to all according to their plans and their views until they collapse in exhaustion. This was never My intent. Instead, they are to carry My love and mercy to those I send them to so My plans are made complete. Beyond this, they are to pay special attention to the needs of the least in My kingdom, their true brothers and sisters. By this, My Body will be built up, and much will be accomplished for the kingdom.

Go where I send you, and do what I ask of you. Spread My love and mercy wherever you go. Take care of the widows and orphans among My people. Visit your brothers and sisters in prison. Give to My people who are needy or strangers among you. Do all of this as I lead, and your reward will be great in heaven.

JULY 26

*Come away by yourselves to a
desolate place and rest a while.*

Mark 6:31

❧

There is a time and a season for every matter under heaven.
This includes periods of great activity and of rest.

I know what it is like to walk upon the earth. I have
experienced times of leanness and times of plenty, times of
sorrow and times of laughter, and times of energy and
times of weariness. I give My children seasons of kingdom
work, and I give them times of rest. I am not a hard
taskmaster as some imagine Me to be. Those who follow Me
closely know this because I tell them when the effort has
been enough and it is time for rest. Those who do their own
works do not know these times of rest because their efforts
of the flesh are never enough.

I know you intimately. I created you. I know when you
need physical rest. I know when your emotions need
unwinding. I know when your spirit needs refreshment.
Listen to Me when I say *enough*. Take time to rejuvenate
your body and soul.

JULY 27

A new commandment I give to you, that you love one another: just as I have loved you, you also are to love one another. By this all people will know that you are my disciples, if you have love for one another.

John 13:34-35

࿇

It is My command that you love one another. This command is specifically for My Church. My love is to be a beacon to all I am calling from the world. My disciples are to let My love shine forth out of the abundance they show to each other.

The world is a skeptical place. It looks for inconsistencies between words and actions. It ridicules My Church for its lack of love and tolerance. It points out the infighting among the various schisms, declaring that even My own people cannot agree on what is truth. The world uses such examples as excuses to discount the message of the Gospel or to declare the irrelevance of My Church. They do not see the love and mercy that should characterize those who claim to be My disciples.

My command to you is not optional. Love your brothers and sisters in My Body! Seek the common ground, and get about the work of the kingdom together. If you cannot demonstrate My love to one another, what do you have to offer to the world?

July 28

I sent you to reap that for which you did not labor. Others have labored, and you have entered into their labor.

John 4:38

❧❦

My kingdom work stretches from generation to generation to the end of the ages. It is not the work of the one but the many. Those who enjoy the harvest reap what others have labored in before them. This is the way of the kingdom of God.

My work on earth leaves no room for arrogance. Even the most successful harvesters have not worked alone in the fields. Many have gone before them. Some have prepared the tools that made the labor possible. Others have planted and watered. Some have tenderly cared for the young plants. I have gone before all of these, making the way possible. My Church grows one heart at a time by the power of the Holy Spirit working in harmony with human hands.

I have called you to My work. It does not matter where I have placed you or what I have given your hands to do. Whatever it is, do it with all joy! Your contribution to My kingdom is the glorious miracle of Me working through you.

JULY 29

*Truly, truly, I say to you, unless a grain of
wheat falls into the earth and dies, it remains
alone; but if it dies, it bears much fruit.*

John 12:24

❧❧

My kingdom is built on sacrifice. First, it was My sacrifice.
Now, it is yours. Each of My disciples is to become more
like Me as we walk together. They are to spend their lives
for the sake of others.

I left an example for My disciples to follow. I came in love.
I dealt in mercy. I sought neither fame nor favor with the
world, only the approval of the One who sent Me. I served
others with patience. I listened with empathy to stories of
pain and despair. I ate with outcasts, accepting them for
what they were and encouraging them in what they could
become. I challenged the hypocrisy of the religious elite and
the earthly kingdoms they had built in God's name. I
reached out My hand to sinners without condemnation. I
gave My life so others might live.

You have only a short time on earth. Invest yourself fully
in the work I give you. Die to yourself, and bring forth much
fruit. A great cloud of witnesses surrounds you, declaring
this to be the way of My kingdom.

JULY 30

If anyone loves me, he will keep my word, and my Father will love him, and we will come to him and make our home with him. Whoever does not love me does not keep my words.

John 14:23-24

৵৶

My disciples follow Me in both word and deed. They are people of faith, rightly putting what they believe into action. They live out My love in their lives. Theirs is the way of mercy.

Many attach themselves to My name, some with sincerity and some under pretense. Those who live as I have asked them to live and do as I have asked them to do show that they love Me. They have allowed Me room in their hearts to live and to work. Those who disregard My clear intent in their lives pay only lip service to Me. These pick and choose among My words and then go their own way. They do not love Me, only themselves. Their choices clearly demonstrate this to be true, though they deceive themselves by thinking otherwise. They make no room for Me in their hearts and resist My work in their lives at every turn.

I did not save you to live apart from you. I reached out to pull you close, becoming *God with you*. Invite Me to dwell fully in your heart and renew it. Ask Me to live through you each day. The world will then see our love for one another.

JULY 31

If anyone serves me, he must follow me; and
where I am, there will my servant be also. If
anyone serves me, the Father will honor him.

John 12:26

કৈન્જ

My disciples follow where I lead. Their desire is to be wherever I am. They seek to join in the work I am doing. Our Father looks down and is pleased.

I can be found in the most unusual places. I am at work in the strangest of circumstances. I go where I need to go and do what I need to do. Those who know Me rejoice wherever they see Me at work. These know I am not bound by the proprieties of man nor fettered by his conventional wisdom. Instead, My servants join Me in unexpected places and work with Me in peculiar circumstances. Their hearts are filled with joy because they are with Me in the work. They care not what others think but seek only My affirmation.

I get My hands dirty in the affairs of mankind. It is here that I call you to work. Everything I do is good and right, and so it is with My servants who work by My side. *Will you join Me regardless of what others may think?*

AUGUST

Fruit and rewards. Result and recompense. These are signs of a life lived for Jesus as His disciple.

AUGUST 1

*I am the vine; you are the branches. Whoever
abides in me and I in him, he it is that bears
much fruit, for apart from me you can do nothing.*

John 15:5

કે≈ૐ

I am rooted in the power of the Godhead. I bring forth life to
all who are attached to Me. This life is eternal and full of My
character. All branches found alive in Me show the growth
of My fruitfulness in them.

Those who abide in Me come alive. These feed from My
spiritual nourishment and take on My characteristics. The
power of eternal life surges through them. Spiritual fruit
buds and develops. These branches grow strong in My
presence and are numbered with the other branches in the
vineyard of My Father. All of this is possible because of
their connection with Me. Without this, nothing good can
come of the branch. It is incapable of producing the type of
fruit I seek.

I live in you, and through Me you have everlasting
viability. Take nourishment from Me. Flourish in My ways.
Grow in the strength of My inexhaustible supply.

AUGUST 2

*Every branch in me that does not bear fruit he [the Father]
takes away, and every branch that does bear fruit he [the
Father] prunes, that it may bear more fruit.*

John 15:2

～◌᷍

My life-giving nourishment is provided with a purpose. Its
many possibilities must be directed and trained into the
vine so the vine may grow and bear fruit for the kingdom.

Pruning is a natural part of growing in the vineyard of
God. It is the cutting away of unprofitable growth. Without
it, a branch will grow wildly in many directions, wasting its
energies in confusion. The Vinedresser trains the branch to
grow in the most profitable way for the kingdom. Useless
diversions are cut away, focusing My nourishment to the
desired result. Unfruitful branches are removed, making
room for the healthy branches to flourish and bear more
fruit.

Every branch that grows in Me experiences the pain of
periodic pruning. Do not lose heart when you see some of
your growth removed. Know that you are being trained and
prepared to bear more good fruit for My kingdom. Before
long, you will see the wisdom of the pruning.

August 3

If anyone does not abide in me he is thrown away
like a branch and withers; and the branches are
gathered, thrown into the fire, and burned.

John 15:6

❦

Those branches that abide in Me live in Me. I have
supernaturally grafted them to the vine. There are others
that have attached themselves to Me but are not grafted in.
These use Me for their purposes and are only superficial
parasitic growths.

Many parasitic vines attach themselves to Me. These
exist only by association and are not true branches. Like
wild grapevines, they clog the vineyard, creating confusion
and robbing My Church of its energy. Many times these
look like genuine branches, but they never bear the
spiritual fruit I seek. The wise among My children will
recognize the seemingly lush growth of these branches
along with the curious lack of spiritual fruit. They will take
steps to keep from being entangled in the tendrils of
deception and smothered by the poisonous foliage of such
branches.

As you grow in the vineyard, beware of false branches.
They will hinder your growth. Ask Me and I will give you
wisdom to see them. I will help you avoid becoming
entangled with them and having your fruitfulness choked
out by them.

AUGUST 4

You did not choose me, but I chose you and
appointed you that you should go and bear
fruit and that your fruit should abide.

John 15:16

࿊

I have chosen you and grafted you onto My vine. I have appointed the times and places for opportunities of fruitfulness in Me.

I have a plan for each of My branches. I have crafted them to bear specific fruits for the kingdom. The wise follow My lead and allow Me to do My work in them. But many forget that *I* have chosen *them*. These adopt an attitude that they are somehow doing Me a favor by being My followers or associating with Me. They take this attitude into the good works they do. They go off on their own and do what seems right in their own eyes, thinking I should be pleased to bless their efforts. Frustration and a lack of fulfillment follow their toiling. The fruit of their works does not last because it does not abide in Me but only in them.

Give yourself over completely to all I have planned for you. Allow My life-giving power to flow through you. I know the fruit you are appointed to bear. It is kingdom fruit. It lives on forever. Let Me bring it forth in your life. You will experience great satisfaction and joy.

AUGUST 5

*By this my Father is glorified, that you bear
much fruit and so prove to be my disciples.*

John 15:8

స్త్రీ

I make great investments in My Father's vineyard. I do this
so He can receive the glory of a bountiful harvest from My
disciples.

My Father gives Me a free hand with My followers. He
watches as I invest time and resources. He sees My patient
work in each life. He knows My noble plans for every child
of Mine. All that is needed is their willing cooperation. If My
children will walk with Me and work with Me, I will make
them fruitful in due season. If they will endure the pruning
and shaping, I will cause them to flourish. Bearing much
fruit is not easy or painless. It is only possible by My power
flowing through each branch. Every branch must consent
to the process of becoming fruitful. Otherwise, there will be
no fruit.

I have plans for a bountiful harvest of lasting fruit in
your life. It is far beyond what you could think or imagine.
*Give Me permission right now to perform My miraculous work
in you so you can bear much fruit.*

AUGUST 6

These things I have spoken to you, that my joy may be in you, and that your joy may be full.

John 15:11

❧❧

Joy is an important fruit in the lives of My children. It is independent of circumstances. It flows from knowing that I am with you each step of the way.

The world is a hostile place. Dangers abound and evil lurks. As My child, walking through all that stands against you and the kingdom life is daunting. Successfully navigating on your own is *impossible*. Despair, turmoil, uncertainty, and fear await all who walk on their own. But I have lifted this burden from you. I have invited you to follow Me. I know what lies ahead and where to lead you each day. I have even told you that I will provide all you need to bear much fruit. Why? To give you hope for the journey so your joy may be full. All that is required is for you to stay in step with Me.

It brings Me great joy to provide all these things for you! Let us walk, and let My joy become yours. Let it overflow your heart and pour out each day as we journey together as friends.

August 7

*So, every healthy tree bears good fruit, but the diseased
tree bears bad fruit. A healthy tree cannot bear bad
fruit, nor can a diseased tree bear good fruit.*

Matthew 7:17-18

≥≥≤

There are many trees growing among My people. Some are
healthy with good fruit and some are diseased with bad
fruit.

Trees have no control over the type of fruit they bear.
What ends up on the branches comes from the nature of
the tree. There can be degrees of quality and quantity, but
the type of tree determines the type of fruit. Healthy trees
cannot produce bad fruit. There may be little fruit to show
for the time and investment involved or it may be of poor
quality, but any fruit will be good because the tree is good.
Likewise, trees that are diseased cannot produce good fruit.
There will always be something wrong with the fruit—
something that doesn't quite taste or look or smell right—
because the tree is diseased.

I know your fruit. It comes from My vine. It is good
because you are good. You are good because you have been
grafted onto My vine, and I am good. Bear your fruit to the
glory of God our Father.

AUGUST 8

Thus you will recognize them by their fruits.

Matthew 7:20

❧

The fruit of each person is true to that person's nature, whether good or bad, healthy or diseased. The key is being able to determine the type of fruit it is—good or bad.

Many do not understand exactly what the *fruit* of a person's life really is. Some say it is a matter of sin—its presence or absence in one's life. This cannot be since there are no sinless people, and a tree is either good or bad. Others say the actions of a person identify their fruit. This is not entirely true because actions, like words, can be deceptive to the unsuspecting. The truth is that fruit is primarily spiritual in nature. It is either rooted in the Holy Spirit or the spirit of antichrist, which is demonic. Because of this, discernment is the key to detecting bad fruit from a diseased tree. Actions can be made to look good, and words can sound sincere, but the Holy Spirit's discernment shines the light of truth on them all.

You have been given the Holy Spirit to help you in this life. Stop and ask Him for discernment. He will give it to you so you can clearly see the fruit of false teachers who are active in the world around you.

AUGUST 9

For out of the abundance of the heart the mouth speaks. The good person out of his good treasure brings forth good, and the evil person out of his evil treasure brings forth evil.

Matthew 12:34-35

❧❧

The heart of each man or woman is a deep well. Out of it are drawn treasures that reflect its nature. It cannot be otherwise. By these treasures, the nature of the heart is revealed.

The foundation of every tree is its root. From there the tree grows and spreads out its branches, eventually bringing forth fruit. It is the same with the heart. The heart is nourished by its root and takes on the root's nature—whether good or diseased. Fruit is then produced from the heart. If a person abides in Me, I am their root. I cleanse their heart so it produces good fruit. If the person does not abide in Me, their root is fleshly and rotten. Their heart remains diseased and so does its fruit.

I pay close attention to your heart. I listen for attitudes and beliefs in your words. Build up a good treasure room in your heart. Remove all that is rotten and dead. Fill it with things that are true, honorable, just, and pure so your speech will be commendable to all.

AUGUST 10

*Not everyone who says to me, 'Lord, Lord,' will
enter the kingdom of heaven, but the one who
does the will of my Father who is in heaven.*

Matthew 7:21

❧❧

I am the Lord over all that is seen and unseen. My Father
gave this position of authority to Me. My children rejoice
because it is so!

My children know My voice. They bow before Me and
rightly call Me their Lord. They do the will of My Father,
which is My will. Many, though, reject My Father's will.
These may associate with Me and My people, but their
hearts are far from Me. They are not of My kingdom but of
another. They are goats among My sheep and weeds among
My wheat. My children may struggle to identify them, but I
know them. Their fruit is not Mine. It is fleshly and
demonic. They do not follow My Father's will but their own.

Do not be deceived by words that tickle your ears or
actions that entertain your flesh. My kingdom is founded
upon the truth that I am the Lord. Tend to your good fruit,
and do not taste of the diseased fruit of others.

AUGUST 11

On that day many will say to me, 'Lord, Lord, did we not prophesy in your name, and cast out demons in your name, and do many mighty works in your name?'

Matthew 7:22

❧

I am the keeper of good fruit. I help My children produce it in their lives. Others are purveyors of diseased fruit, hawking it as though it were good and acceptable.

Mankind knows of their guilt. They try to make amends through good works. But these are not sufficient. Such fruit is of their own making, the work of their own efforts. Though they label it as Mine and profess to grow it in My name, it is diseased and rotten inside. The Holy Spirit did not produce it. It is the work of their hands alone. The demons delight in this counterfeit fruit. By it, they deceive many and drag them off to share their fate of coming judgment. All fruit that is not produced by Me will stand as a testimony against its owners on the last day.

My child, do not be like those who are not of My kingdom. They strive to produce fruit on their own and then ask Me to bless it. Instead, remember you are Mine, and My power is alive in you. Produce fruit worthy of your eternal inheritance by living for Me and in Me.

AUGUST 12

And then will I declare to them, 'I never knew you;
depart from me, you workers of lawlessness.'

Matthew 7:23

❧

I will sentence the lawless to eternal destruction, but the righteous will live with Me forever. This is just, and it is true.

Those who do not bear My fruit and instead bear their own are workers of lawlessness. They have done what is right in their own eyes from a heart of rebellion. They do not know Me, and I do not know them. They will not share in the inheritance of the righteous who know Me and do My will. Instead, they will take their place in the lake of fire with their father, the devil. Many will cry out to Me on that day and profess their allegiance, but I know of their treachery against Me. I will gaze upon the sinful fruit of their iniquity and turn away from them for all eternity.

Rejoice that you are not numbered with the unrighteous! You are Mine, and I love you! Bask in My love, and let it wash over you like a warm wave. Your inheritance is sure in My kingdom. Your fruit will be celebrated throughout eternity.

AUGUST 13

A man had a fig tree planted in his vineyard, and he
came seeking fruit on it and found none. And he said
to the vinedresser, 'Look, for three years now I have
come seeking fruit on this fig tree, and I find none.
Cut it down. Why should it use up the ground?'

Luke 13:6-7

❧❧

The justice of My Father demands that an account be given
for every life lived. He carefully considers the fruit of each
tree, looking to see what has become of His longsuffering.

For everyone, there is a day of reckoning. Because My
Father is holy, He cannot simply overlook sin. Many in the
world expect Him to do so, but He will not. Those who do
not bear righteous fruit do not belong to Me. These will be
judged on the last day and cast into the lake of fire. Their
rebellion will testify against them. My children will also give
an account. They will not be judged as sinners because
they have been covered by My sacrifice of blood and have
taken on My righteousness. Instead, I will judge them by
the amount of fruit produced in their lives as compared to
My investment in them. They will be rewarded according to
this judgment.

You have been redeemed. I rejoice over the fruit you
allow Me to produce in your life as I continue to invest in
you. My earnest desire is for you to be found with much
fruit on that day when you stand before Me. Forsake
worldly gain, which is temporary. Instead, bear much fruit
and gain rewards that never perish.

August 14

And he answered him, 'Sir, let it alone this year also, until I dig around it and put on manure. Then if it should bear fruit next year, well and good; but if not, you can cut it down.'

Luke 13:8-9

་ཤ་

Our Father is patient. He sent Me into the world to work, and He gives Me time to do so. I am also patient. I work to produce fruit—first of repentance and then of righteousness.

Many mistake the patience of a loving God for His excusing of their sin. They point to the years that pass and the lack of righteous judgment upon the deeds of mankind as proof. They do not understand that I am at work digging, watering, and fertilizing. What they see as a time of reprieve is actually a time of accruing judgment. On that day when My patience fails, these will see that they are without excuse. They will be judged for the lack of righteous fruit from their rebellious hearts. My love and mercy are great but judgment will come.

Your short time of life on earth is precious to Me. Do not go the way of the world and abuse My patient mercy in your life. Instead, allow Me to break your heart with My love and bring forth fruits of repentance and righteousness in your life. *Let us begin today.*

AUGUST 15

A sower went out to sow.

Matthew 13:3

❧

I am always at work. Through the Holy Spirit, I sow the truths of My kingdom in the hearts of mankind.

The heart of man is complex soil. One day it is receptive and fertile. The next, it is hard and stony. Sometimes it is free of weeds, and other times it is choked with thorns. It is into these various conditions that I faithfully sow My truths. It is out of these same conditions that I await the fruits of My labors. As long as a heart is rooted in Me, its potential for fruit bearing is tremendous. The key to a harvest is to allow Me to till the soil of the heart, clearing out the rocks and the thorns and breaking up its hardness.

Your heart is My field. Allow Me to do My great work in it. I can only prepare it for My truths to the extent you will allow. Decide to give Me access today! I am ready to work, and I have My seeds of truth with Me.

AUGUST 16

*When anyone hears the word of the kingdom
and does not understand it, the evil one comes
and snatches away what has been sown in his
heart. This is what was sown along the path.*

Matthew 13:19

☙❧

Just as I am always at work, so is the evil one. He sends his demons to snatch My truths out of your heart.

A hard heart is the devil's playground. He knows this type of soil will resist all attempts of penetration by My truths. He makes sure the soil remains trampled and hard-packed. He uses wounds, disappointment, and sin to keep it so. He relies on pride and rebellion to guard against all attempts to soften and break up the soil. He makes sure it is regularly picked clean of any good seed that is sown. *Does this sound like the condition of your heart?*

My precious one, do not allow your heart to become hard and barren. Instead, let Me water it with My living water and till it with the Holy Spirit. I can break your heart so you can be healed. All I need is your permission to do so. *Will you give it?*

AUGUST 17

*As for what was sown on rocky ground, this is the one
who hears the word and immediately receives it with
joy, yet he has no root in himself, but endures for a
while, and when tribulation or persecution arises on
account of the word, immediately he falls away.*

Matthew 13:20-21

৵৶

Good soil is the result of preparation. It is easy to scratch
the surface, but great effort is required to plow and to till.

Rocky ground is the result of an unprepared heart.
Instead of the richness found in the deepness of the soil,
only the dusty surface is made available for the seed. It is
the result of a lack of commitment and the laziness that
accompanies this attitude. Instead of digging deep into the
heart and hauling away all that is unprofitable, its owner
makes a shallow survey and only what is easy to deal with
is disturbed. Such scratching merely stirs up the dust,
never exposing the real issues of one's life or the fertile soil
necessary to produce fruit from the truths I sow.

Do not grieve the Holy Spirit. Instead, let Him dig deep
and show you the things that are displeasing to Me so they
can be removed from your life. I have a rich crop planned
for your life. *Will you grant Me permission to work?*

AUGUST 18

*As for what was sown among thorns, this is
the one who hears the word, but the cares
of the world and the deceitfulness of riches
choke the word, and it proves unfruitful.*

Matthew 13:22

৵৹

Thorns are noise. They grow readily in the world. They are dense, happily taking all of the available nutrients from the soil and diminishing the light so nothing else can grow.

The world is a noise-filled place. Most of its inhabitants do not realize what it has done to them. Distractions come from every direction. There is always something vying for their attention. The heart has preferences, and the world has a steady supply of noise to feed them. Some of these preferences are not bad in themselves, while others are. Nevertheless, all of them can quickly take on a life of their own as obsessions. In no time, the soil of the heart has a rich crop of thorny weeds. These consume all available time, attention, and desire. Any seeds that get through to the soil are quickly smothered and choked.

It is time to simplify your life. If you will sit quietly before Me and listen for My voice, I will show you all the noises of the world in your life that keep you from a successful walk with Me. You must put some of your preferences aside and take up some of My priorities, but this is the way of a disciple, is it not? *What preferences do you need to exchange for My priorities?*

AUGUST 19

As for what was sown on good soil, this is the one
who hears the word and understands it. He indeed
bears fruit and yields, in one case a hundredfold, in
another sixty, and in another thirty.

Matthew 13:23

൙൙

Good soil makes good fruit possible. The seeds of My truth
can flourish in it and yield much fruit.

The hearts of My children are My focus. I know that if I
have one's heart I also have their will. Because of this, I
invest much in the heart of each of My followers. To the
extent they will yield, I can do My work. Preparing good soil
for a crop is a process. There is no instant formula for
success. Instead, the key to good soil is the discipline of a
close daily walk with Me. The result of such a walk is a
fruitful life for My children, one that brings glory to My
Father and leaves the world speechless.

Your heart is like a fertile field that stretches out before
Me. I can already see the bountiful crop of fruit. Walk with
Me, and work with Me. Together, we will watch it come to
pass. *Are you ready to do as I ask?*

AUGUST 20

*Do not lay up for yourselves treasures on earth, where moth
and rust destroy and where thieves break in and steal.*

Matthew 6:19

❧

I know the plans I have for you. I also know the steps
necessary and the order in which they must be taken. I
even know the eternal rewards these could bring. But the
real question is this: *What is your objective in this life?*

This is one of the most important questions My children
should ask themselves—both early in their walk with Me
and periodically along the way. Yet, few stop long enough to
ask. Without a clear vision for what I have planned for
them—their calling—many struggle to find a balance
between the things of the world and the things on My mind.
It is here where the shiny objects of the world begin to set
the agenda for their lives—careers, possessions, fortunes,
and retirements. Soon, a life has been consumed in the
scramble to attain these things and to keep them secure in
an uncertain world. And what is left at the end of it all? A
legacy that has little eternal value.

My child, this life is not *the life* and the next is not *the
afterlife.* Do not be deceived. You begin to really live after
your short time on earth is over. Whatever you have done of
heavenly value is rewarded. Unlike your earthly estate,
these rewards last forever.

AUGUST 21

But lay up for yourselves treasures in heaven,
where neither moth nor rust destroys and
where thieves do not break in and steal.

Matthew 6:20

❧

Where I am, there is security. What I protect is kept safe.
My reward reserves cannot be exhausted.

There is no true security in the world. Few things of any
value can be counted on. As the world careens toward its
sure end, this becomes even more certain. Change is the
only constant that lies ahead. Even so, how much effort do
My children pour into accumulating and preserving earthly
things! They have confused priorities. This world is not
their home. They pass quickly through it like a shadow
passes on a sunny day. Heaven is their true home. Their
time there never ceases. What will they take with them from
this life? What will they have accumulated in the next?
These are weighty questions that require your serious
consideration.

It is time to gain a heavenly perspective. After all, you
will spend the rest of eternity there. What rewards will you
enjoy? What position will you have? Where will you sit at
the feast table? It is not too late to begin walking with Me
and securing these eternal treasures. I promise that these
will be more magnificent than anything the world has to
offer to you.

August 22

For where your treasure is, there will your heart be also.

Luke 12:34

৵৽

Treasures are the desires of the heart. Every heart has desires. It is a question of the nature of these desires. *Are yours temporal or are they eternal?*

The human heart was created to be filled by a close relationship with Me. Desires were to be focused and prioritized through this relationship, providing harmony to human life. This was disrupted by sin. Now, priorities are confused. The *present* easily occupies the place of the *eternal*. The drive for possessions, power, or prestige fills the hearts of many. What can be seen and grasped has replaced faith in what must be believed and hoped for. The fleeting moments of the present have been given more value than the unending eons of eternity.

Remember, My child, things of value are pursued while the unimportant is passed by. Take an inventory of the treasures you are chasing. There, you will find your heart.

AUGUST 23

*No servant can serve two masters, for either he will hate the
one and love the other, or he will be devoted to the one and
despise the other. You cannot serve God and money.*

Luke 16:13

❧

Idols are objects of devotion that have a place of priority in
the human heart. Many things can become idols in this
world, but each shares a common characteristic—they
represent the choosing of a false god over Me and the
priorities of another kingdom over Mine.

I am the Master of My kingdom. Satan is the master of
his. The goals of each kingdom are exhibited in the
priorities of its servants. Those who serve Me walk by the
Holy Spirit. Those who serve Satan walk in the flesh.
Attitudes, thoughts, words, and actions reveal which
master is being served in the moment. Many of My children
move easily between masters. They fail to see that they
serve either Me or Satan in every moment of their lives,
advancing My kingdom or sustaining his. Every double-
minded child of Mine must stop and ponder what they are
doing. They cannot love us both. Their devotion for one of
us will fail. Everyone has a master. *Are you serving your
Master or another?*

When you were brought into My kingdom by salvation, I
began to pursue your heart with great passion to make it
Mine. Choose Me in every moment of your life. Do not
become double-minded, having a divided heart.

AUGUST 24

*Fear not, little flock, for it is your Father's good
pleasure to give you the kingdom.*

Luke 12:32

❧

My Father wants each of Our children to experience the
fullness of the kingdom. This means an abundance in Me
during this life and great treasures in the next.

Many do not understand what having 'abundant life'
means. These quickly assume it to mean material blessings
and places of privilege as My child. This type of thinking
breeds all manner of false doctrines concerning prosperity
within My Church. Covetousness and greed do not
discriminate between those who are lost and those who are
Mine. They are the same sins for all who practice them.
True abundance is found in My continual presence during
our walk together through this life. Such a fruitful life here
on earth leads to a life of many treasures in the next.

Life in My kingdom begins here on earth for you. Walk
with Me along its path. Your heart will overflow with My
abundance. Your treasures in heaven will overflow your
treasury.

August 25

Sell your possessions, and give to the needy. Provide
yourselves with moneybags that do not grow old,
with a treasure in the heavens that does not fail,
where no thief approaches and no moth destroys.

Luke 12:33

☙❧

Abundance in the kingdom is found by fulfilling your calling
here on earth. This is possible for all who will walk with Me
and do what I ask of them.

Each of My children has a distinct calling. What I have
planned for one is not exactly the same as I have planned
for another. This is by design. It brings vibrancy to My
kingdom by avoiding the well-traveled rut of conformity. As
you fulfill your calling, you bear the fruit I intended. You
also build up heavenly rewards according to what you have
done with what I have given to you. This is the way of the
kingdom.

Do not worry about what I am having others do for My
kingdom. Remain focused on what I am having you do. I am
not the God of the herd but the God of the individual. I
have a plan I have called you to. It allows you to fulfill your
purpose, which is to bring glory to our Father.

AUGUST 26

The one who receives a prophet because he is a prophet will receive a prophet's reward, and the one who receives a righteous person because he is a righteous person will receive a righteous person's reward. And whoever gives one of these little ones even a cup of cold water because he is a disciple, truly, I say to you, he will by no means lose his reward.

Matthew 10:41-42

❧❧

Rewards in heaven are as varied as the acts on earth that accrue them. They are not given as motives for action but as honors for proper motives during this life. Love for Me is the motive. *Understand what this means.*

A disciple follows his or her teacher and becomes more like the teacher. A disciple learns by doing what the teacher does. A disciple's motivation is pure—to bring honor to the teacher above all else. I give My disciples eternal rewards for their service to Me. I have purposefully separated these honors from their associated actions by death. This delay preserves the pure motivation of obedience to Me. Nevertheless, it is not wrong for My children to look forward to enjoying their rewards for all of eternity. I think on these rewards often, anticipating the great joy these will bring to each who will receive them.

I have great plans for you in heaven! I have special honors and gifts to bestow for your life lived in My service. You cannot imagine what it will be like to enjoy them forevermore. I am so excited!

August 27

*Behold, I am coming soon, bringing my recompense
with me, to repay each one for what he has done.*

Revelation 22:12

❧

The date of My return marches ever nearer, and time grows
short for all the people of the earth. Each will be judged by
their fruit, and each will be rewarded accordingly.

All of My children share My gift of salvation equally.
There are no degrees of eternal life. One either has it by
faith in Me or does not. There are, however, degrees of
rewards and honors. These are based on each believer's
fruit as compared to what they were provided with in this
life. Some are given little to work with in this life, and their
fruit will be judged accordingly. Others are given much, and
for these there is an expectation of abundant fruit. My
Father determined the circumstances of their lives and how
much they were given. I determine how much they will
receive as recompense.

I look expectantly for fruit in your life. I know the
opportunities you were given and the obstacles in your way.
I have seen both your privileges and challenges. I have
walked with you and invested in you, freely giving of Myself.
Will I see fruit worthy of what you were given?

AUGUST 28

And everyone who has left houses or brothers or sisters or
father or mother or children or lands, for my name's sake,
will receive a hundredfold and will inherit eternal life.

Matthew 19:29

❧❧

It costs much to follow Me in this life. Family, friends, and
opportunities—the sacrifice goes on and on. Yet, I will repay
each one for their sacrifice.

Those who follow close after Me know the price of laying
down their lives each day. These have left loved ones and
acquaintances behind to follow Me. They have given over
their careers and their plans in order to be used as I have
planned. They have sacrificially given of their finances and
their possessions. I have seen all that has been done out of
love for Me. It will be replaced many times over in heaven.
There will be much rejoicing over the exchange of the
meager and temporary for the ample and eternal.

I know what you have given. I know precisely what it
cost. One day, I will generously replace it all...forever. Do
not focus on the sacrifice. Instead, look at all I have done in
you and through you, and rejoice!

AUGUST 29

In my Father's house are many rooms. If it were not so,
would I have told you that I go to prepare a place for you?

John 14:2

≈◦≈

By the time they pass from this life to eternity, each of My
children has a place prepared for them in heaven. The type
of place and its location depend on the fruitfulness of their
lives in service to Me.

Some have heard they will receive a mansion. Others
believe it is just a room like every other room in heaven. I
will only tell you that it is not as most think it to be. It is
true that each person has a place. However, the type, size,
appointments, and proximity to heaven's throne room vary
according to that person's works for Me after becoming My
follower. This dwelling place is one of the rewards I honor
each of My children with based on their fruitfulness while
on earth.

Your place in heaven is under consideration. With every
step along the path, you are shaping its final state. Let us
walk briskly to the tasks I have for you. Let Me work freely
in your heart. The time for faithfulness and fruitfulness is
at hand.

AUGUST 30

His master said to him, 'Well done, good and faithful
servant. You have been faithful over a little; I will set
you over much. Enter into the joy of your master.'

Matthew 25:21

৵৵

Each of My children enters into My joy in heaven. All tears
are wiped away. Regrets are forgotten. Sorrows are replaced
with gladness and singing.

Joy finds its completion in heaven for each of My
children. On the day of their arrival, I hand them their
rewards and bestow upon them their honors. No matter
how slight or how bountiful these are, each one walks the
streets with great joy as they take up their place in heaven.
Everyone is given an assignment. Some have a singular
task to do. Others are appointed over many things. The
scope of their eternal occupation is determined by their
faithfulness in what they were given on earth.

I long to welcome you to heaven at the end of your
pilgrim journey on earth. On that day, it will give Me great
pleasure to commend your work according to My will on
earth and to appoint you with a heavenly task. Until then, I
encourage you to run the race set before you with
endurance.

AUGUST 31

And people will come from east and west, and
from north and south, and recline at table in the
kingdom of God. And behold, some are last who
will be first, and some are first who will be last.

Luke 13:29-30

☙❧

In heaven, there will be feasting such as the world has
never seen. All who have entered down through the years
will be there.

All of My children join Me at My feast table, but not all
are seated close to Me. I sit at the head of the table, and the
seats of the saints stretch down either side as far as the eye
can see. These seats and places of honor are based on each
person's faithfulness in serving Me during this short life on
earth. The wise will understand that fruitfulness on earth
has eternal ramifications.

At My table in heaven, all of the Old Covenant saints will
join together with those of this age for times of joyous
feasting and fellowship. The closeness of your seat to Me
will be determined by your closeness to Me in this life.
Where will you be seated?

SEPTEMBER

Jesus walked the dusty tracks of this world. He received ridicule. He endured persecution. He suffered pain. He overcame hate with His love.

SEPTEMBER 1

A disciple is not above his teacher, nor a servant above his master. It is enough for the disciple to be like his teacher, and the servant like his master. If they have called the master of the house Beelzebub, how much more will they malign those of his household.

Matthew 10:24-25

৵৶

It is My high calling that My disciples should become more like Me. They will share in My glory, but first they must lay their lives down as I have.

I do not call My disciples to endure more than I have in this world. I do not expect them to surpass Me in ridicule or tribulation. But each who would follow Me must know the journey they are undertaking—both its glorious highs and faith shattering lows. Many will speak of warm sheltered pastures heavy with dew-covered grass, but few will reveal the desolate places of persecution that are sure to come to all who are faithful in My ways. I warn My disciples beforehand so their steps may be affirmed and their faith strengthened when they encounter such times. These will not be surprised but will stand immovable in that day.

My child, I endured much to bring light into the world. I now call you out of the shadows to walk in My steps. Do not be dismayed when persecutions strike, but stand tall with confidence! The One who holds your hand has overcome all the world could bring against Him.

SEPTEMBER 2

For he [Jesus] will be delivered over to the Gentiles and will be mocked and shamefully treated and spit upon.

Luke 18:32

❧

When I laid My life down for you, I willingly allowed Myself to suffer persecution. As My follower, you are not immune to the same type of treatment as you lay your life down for Me.

Many of My children think themselves above suffering at the hands of evil in the world. These believe they should live a life of prosperity and ease because they are children of the King. They become indignant when persecutions arise. They fight back in anger and hate as if they own some divine right to avoid such treatment. I tell you plainly, such thoughts are nothing more than the prideful deception of human reasoning. All who faithfully follow Me will taste the bitterness of the world's hatred of Me. For these, times will come when their peacefulness is met with turbulence, their kindness with cruelty, and their acceptance with disdain. What the world has done to their Master will also be done to them.

Will you walk with Me through the gates of Gethsemane? Will you prepare yourself for whatever we are to pass along the way? Will you purpose to remain faithful to the One who has been faithful to you? Take My hand, and let us go.

SEPTEMBER 3

*If the world hates you, know that it
has hated me before it hated you.*

John 15:18

࿎

There is little love for Me in the world. I find widespread
resistance to My ways. Yet, I walk boldly on, confident in
My mission. My faithful followers are with Me.

The world stands against Me in rebellion. It is threatened
by My power over hearts once darkened by sin. Reactions of
its people range from reluctant tolerance to murderous
hatred. My children experience the full spectrum of this
resistance as they walk among the many people of the
earth. Behind each pushback, enmity lurks. And behind
this, the hate-filled spirit of antichrist is at work. Hatred is
a strong emotion. Its ruthlessness knows no bounds. I have
endured it from the Garden of Eden until now. I have
conquered it with love and mercy.

Just as the hatred of the world is boundless, so My love
for you is without end. I have called you out from the
darkness of hate into the light of My love. I will walk with
you through the deathly shadows of this world and into the
verdant pastures that await. *Will you come along?*

September 4

*If you were of the world, the world would love you as its
own; but because you are not of the world, but I chose
you out of the world, therefore the world hates you.*

John 15:19

❧

The world loves its own and holds them close. It hates all
who are Mine because I have snatched them out of its
hand.

The world is obsessed with reigning over its own. It
jealously guards them against My truths. It is zealous in its
opposition to Me. It is adamant in its hatred of all who defy
its ways. Yet, the world woos My children back to itself. It
speaks comforting words of familiarity in their ears. It
promises that I will not notice their turning back to its
ways. It convinces them that I have not forbidden them to
taste of its fruit. As it was with Satan in the Garden, so it is
with him today. His songs of love to My beloved conceal his
true intent for them. He knows they have been called out
from his lair. His last resort is to make them of little use to
Me. His hatred of Me drives his actions.

The world is not your home. It may seem to love you, but
it cannot because you are Mine. Its smile hides fangs
hungry for your heart. Hear the hatred in its voice, and run
far from its clutches. Mine is the voice of true love. My arms
are your protection. Remain with Me. Do not stray.

SEPTEMBER 5

*Remember the word that I said to you: 'A
servant is not greater than his master.' If they
persecuted me, they will also persecute you. If
they kept my word, they will also keep yours.*

John 15:20

❧

The world keeps its own counsel and rejects Mine. It cannot bear the truth or those who proclaim it.

The ways of the world are set, its patterns forged in opposition to Me. My truth is considered foolish and those who live by it, fools. This is why I was mocked and why you will be as well. I call the world to account and am hated for doing so. As you proclaim My truth, you share in this hatred. Do not expect the world to heed your words. It will not. Only those who are called out of the world will hear and respond. These will know it is My voice speaking to them and will recognize My truth. So go where I send you, and speak to those who are there. The Holy Spirit will work, and those who hear will be snatched from the world's grasp.

The world does not tolerate My truth. Remember this. Do not be dismayed or discouraged. Go and do the works I have for you. Watch for the harvest as those who will be Mine gladly receive My truth. Together, we will rejoice over our labors.

September 6

But all these things they will do to you on account of my name, because they do not know him who sent me.

John 15:21

༷

I represent My Father to the world. Those who will not recognize His authority also reject His Messenger. My ambassadors to the world can expect the same treatment.

When I am rejected, it is because My Father is being rejected. Those who refuse subjection to My authority do so because they will not be brought under His. As My representatives, you will likewise be rejected because you submit to My authority in all matters. Those who do not know Me will argue that your submission is illegitimate and not for them. They will violently resist every human attempt to cause them to submit. It is only by the working of the Holy Spirit that these will bow a knee to Me in this life. *Hear and understand what I am saying to you.*

Accept that you will suffer rejection in the world because it does not know Me or the One who sent Me. But you know Me and are known by Me. The Father loves you as one of His own because you have been reborn in Me.

September 7

As you [the Father] sent me into the world,
so I have sent them into the world.

John 17:18

❧

I was sent into the world to fulfill My Father's plans for the world. I knew the hostility I would face, yet I went willingly.

I have been dealing with mankind since our days together in the Garden of Eden. From then until now, I have walked among rebellious people. I have felt the sting of their rejection and their hatred toward the One who created them. I have sent you into this same world. Do not be surprised by what you experience at the hands of the people you are sent among. Instead, expect it. For what else can a sinner do but sin or a rebellious one do but rebel? As you walk through all you must endure, remember that I did not send you out alone. I am with you.

I have chosen you for special assignments in this hostile world. I go before you and come along behind as you execute the plans I have for you. Go as one who is sent with the power of God—boldly, confidently, and expectantly.

SEPTEMBER 8

I do not ask that you take them out of the world,
but that you keep them from the evil one.

John 17:15

༄༅

I know the plans I have for you. Your adversaries can see what I am doing through you. They come to oppose you, resisting My plan each step of the way.

You are involved in a great spiritual battle. You do not fight against flesh and blood as so many of My children have come to believe. Your true enemy is Satan and all of his evil demons. Your calling is your overall assignment. Your walk with Me is the daily battle plan. I will keep you from destruction as we walk along the way. I will be your sure shield. My plans for you in this battle are set. They will stand even if you reject them. Those who will not come along with Me but go their own way do not share in My promise of protection. The evil one waits for permission to steal, kill, and destroy.

My plans take you through enemy territory. Stay with Me and do not reject your calling. I am your shield. As I lead you into the conflict, leave the results to Me. We will celebrate our experiences throughout eternity with those who have gone before you.

September 9

I tell you, my friends, do not fear those who kill the body,
and after that have nothing more that they can do. But I will
warn you whom to fear: fear him who, after he has killed,
has authority to cast into hell. Yes, I tell you, fear him!

Luke 12:4-5

❧

The fear of your God is only the beginning of wisdom.
Thriving in His love and mercy brings wisdom full circle.

Many of My children walk in fear each day. Theirs is not
the fear of reverence for God but the fear of man. Those
who practice such fear do not realize they have put mere
men in My rightful place. It is true that those who are
against Me in this world can do much evil toward My
children. They can ridicule and shun. They can pass laws
to restrict good and promote evil. They can persecute and
throw into prison. They can hurt or even kill. Yet, they
cannot take away the eternal life I give to My children.

I have given you the ability to walk confidently through
the many dangers of this world. You have already laid your
life down before Me. You now have nothing to lose and
much to gain. So do not fear men. Walk boldly with Me.

September 10

Are not five sparrows sold for two pennies? And not one of them is forgotten before God. Why, even the hairs of your head are all numbered. Fear not; you are of more value than many sparrows.

Luke 12:6-7

❧

I am the God of the living. I am the God of the present. I know all who are Mine. I walk with them through their tribulations.

Many of My children live in fear for their futures. They see only what they can see and imagine the rest. They know the world around them is dangerous. They understand that their calling requires them to walk in the midst of this hostility. Many times, they cannot even see where to place their foot for the next step. But I know what is around them. I see what is ahead. I call to each of My children and ask only one thing from them—to take the next step with Me. I do not require faith for the journey, only for the day.

You are a treasured possession. You are of priceless value. I know the details of your life. Nothing escapes My notice. Rest in this knowledge. Let Me lead you over the troubled waters. Allow your confidence in My love for you to cast out all fear.

SEPTEMBER 11

Go, for he [Saul] is a chosen instrument of mine to carry my name before the Gentiles and kings and the children of Israel. For I will show him how much he must suffer for the sake of my name.

Acts 9:15-16

☙❧

All who will follow Me in the kingdom will suffer for the sake of My name. And afterward, I receive them into My glory.

I do not save My children so they can sit idly in the kingdom, waiting for this life to pass. I save them to walk with Me through the world, making an impact for the kingdom. For some, the tasks are small, bringing them only into occasional struggle with the world. For others, the sacrifice is great because the calling is difficult and the conflict is significant. In every case, My grace is sufficient for the challenges of the walk. In My strength, each can succeed in fulfilling their destiny in this life.

As we walk together through your calling, I will show you what you must suffer for Me. I look for a willing heart that follows where I lead and endures to the end. I will then give you the crown of life with great celebration.

SEPTEMBER 12

Truly, I say to you, this poor widow has put in more than all those who are contributing to the offering box. For they all contributed out of their abundance, but she out of her poverty has put in everything she had, all she had to live on.

Mark 12:43-44

❧

What can man give to Me in exchange for My gift of salvation? There is only one thing sufficient—a life fully committed to Me in love out of a deep appreciation for what I have done.

Many serve Me out of convenience. These give Me what is easy to part with from their abundance—time, money, and possessions. Their gifts may be large in quantity, but they are small in personal cost to them. Their sacrifice is minimal and does not accomplish what I desire in their lives. Others have learned to hold their lives and possessions loosely in their hands. These make available whatever I require of them in the moment, regardless of the cost to them. Their commitment to Me is complete. They listen for My voice and do what I ask with a willing heart. Because of this, I can use them to accomplish much.

I have saved you from eternal destruction. Open your hand in gratitude, and give to Me all I ask of you in this short life. Let your attitude be one of joy and not grudging compulsion, knowing that you are being used for the kingdom.

SEPTEMBER 13

Let not your hearts be troubled, neither let them be afraid.

John 14:27

৵৽

Every calling from Me comes into conflict with a resisting world. This is the nature of the kingdom of light piercing the kingdom of darkness.

As the trajectory of their calling is made known to each of My children, the price of following Me in this world is revealed to them. It is here where fear creeps in, robbing many of their confidence and troubling their hearts. This is a necessary process for all who would follow Me. Each must come to the place where they recognize their insufficiency for the tasks ahead. Some will turn from their calling and run to the comfort of the old and familiar. Others will grasp more tightly to My hand and walk on, confident that My strength is sufficient to sustain them through every trial. *What will you do?*

Run quickly to the end of yourself and your capabilities. Once there, cry out to Me. I will answer you and give abundantly of My peace and My strength. We will walk confidently into your future, one step at a time.

SEPTEMBER 14

Behold, I am sending you out as sheep in the midst of wolves, so be wise as serpents and innocent as doves.

Matthew 10:16

❧

I know the ways of the world. Even so, I send My sheep out among its wolves. It is here that they must do the works I have for them to do.

The wolves of the world come against My people with intentional hostility. They seek to intimidate all who are Mine and drive them far from what I have called them to do. The wise conduct themselves shrewdly as they walk among the wolves. These understand the purposeful nature of their opponent's actions and meet their tactics with a calm spirit. They do not turn on the wolves with like fury but instead remain righteous in their walk.

I will give you My wisdom as you walk along the way in the midst of the wolves. Allow mercy and love to reign in your heart, not anger and hostility. This way, you avoid unnecessary troubles and show the world you are Mine.

SEPTEMBER 15

But to what shall I compare this generation? It is like children sitting in the marketplaces and calling to their playmates, 'We played the flute for you, and you did not dance; we sang a dirge, and you did not mourn.'

Matthew 11:16-17

❧

The world is a place of confusion. Its fickle people are tossed to and fro by every trendy wave.

The people of the world thrash about endlessly. They are driven by base passions and whims that know no end. They would have all believe that they hold the moral high ground, but theirs is the religion of self, and each sits on the throne of their life. As My children journey through such a place, they must remain steadfast in their walk. Running off in attempts to placate the crowds with demonstrations of worldly relevance leads only to wasted lives of futility. Instead, My followers are to walk in My unchanging truth. It is always relevant.

Do not get caught up trying to become relevant to the world by following the latest fad or trend of worldly wisdom. Remain relevant by demonstrating My love in the face of hate and My mercy in the face of cruelty. Those who I am calling will see this as truth and be drawn to its source.

SEPTEMBER 16

*For John came neither eating nor drinking, and they
say, 'He has a demon.' The Son of Man came eating
and drinking, and they say, 'Look at him! A glutton
and a drunkard, a friend of tax collectors and
sinners!' Yet wisdom is justified by her deeds.*

Matthew 11:18-19

❧

The demands of the world are insatiable. The restlessness
of its people defies conformity.

It is impossible for those who walk with Me to satisfy the
expectations of the world. Fault will be found with every
action as its holy motive is questioned. Righteousness can
find no peace with evil, nor can truth with deception. One
act will be criticized and another ridiculed. The wise among
My children understand and accept this. They do not try to
placate through compromise, nor do they seek to avoid
persecution by conforming to the ways of the world.
Instead, they speak My truth in love and extend My mercy
generously.

You wrestle against demonic rulers of darkness in this
world. They will not be placated. Remain true to Me and the
calling I have given you. Live a life of substance for the
kingdom.

September 17

See that no one leads you astray.

Matthew 24:4

ॐ‿ॐ

I am executing My Father's plans with a singleness of purpose. I will not be deterred from My work in the world. I have called you to join with Me in this labor of love. Stand steadfast in your calling.

The world rejects Me and resists My work. It wants no interference in its ways. Its turmoil refuses My peace, and My healing balm is spurned by its masses. The world also seeks to thwart the impact of My Church. It alternates its use of fear and lust to lead My people astray. Intimidation and the threat of suffering make many turn away from their work. Others are lured by worldly pleasures or the acclaim and praise of man. These are brought into captivity by their fleshly desires and kept from the true work I intended for them. Any of My sheep that are led astray leave their Shepherd and join with the goats aligned against Him.

You belong to My flock. Keep your eyes on Me, your Shepherd. Do not allow yourself to be turned aside by intimidation or desire. Your calling is of great importance to Me and a source of My delight.

SEPTEMBER 18

*And you will hear of wars and rumors of wars. See
that you are not alarmed, for this must take place,
but the end is not yet. For nation will rise against
nation, and kingdom against kingdom, and there
will be famines and earthquakes in various places.
All these are but the beginning of the birth pains.*

Matthew 24:6-8

⌒⌒

I walk on the water in the midst of the storm. I call My
children out of the familiarity of their boats to come and
walk with Me.

Agitation is a hallmark of the world. It has been so since
the entrance of sin and will continue until the end. Man's
inhumanity to man has been a constant theme as deep
stirrings of hatred and greed reign in the hearts of many.
The earth, too, groans under the weight of sin. It shakes
and roars while it awaits the day of its redemption. The end
is not yet, but it will come soon enough. Walk with Me on
the water in the midst of the storm. Do not fret over the
waves that foam around you or you will sink into their
darkness. Come with Me. We will find the way between the
mighty billows.

It is easy to be overcome by the magnitude of the world's
troubles. Day after day these beat against the security of
your boat. Yet, I have called you to leave your boat behind
and walk on the very water of these storms. *Will you step
out in faith?*

SEPTEMBER 19

And then many will fall away and betray
one another and hate one another.

Matthew 24:10

༄

Persecution is a great sifter of all who identify with Me. It separates the true wheat from the false chaff.

Many profess to follow Me while the road is level and smooth. These enjoy their association with My people and with Me. When persecutions come, however, many of them fall away and go back to their old lives. The lie of their professed love for Me is exposed by their lack of commitment and the betrayal of My ways. For these, the cost of being a disciple is too great. It was never in their hearts to go where I led. My true disciples stay the course. They may falter for a season, but they will rise again and walk with Me. Their hearts are Mine.

Take My hand and walk with Me through the difficult days. If you stumble, I will pick you up. When you are weary, I will give you rest. Your heart belongs to Me. I will give you strength.

September 20

And because lawlessness will be increased,
the love of many will grow cold.

Matthew 24:12

❧

Rebellion lurks under every lawless deed. This rebellion is against Me. It brings danger and persecution to My people.

The faith of each of My children is tested during times of lawlessness. Many lose their zeal for following Me as self-preservation causes them to reconsider our walk together. Some grow faint in the fires of persecution and pull back. Others run to avoid the flames altogether. Those who do such things reject My call to stand firm. Their love of self overcomes their love for Me. But My true disciples persevere. They hold more tightly to My hand as the heat is turned up.

Be zealous for Me. Do not let persecutions quench the fire of your love. I stand ever ready to help you remain steadfast through the trials of life, just as I did for each of My children in the fiery furnace and the lion's den.

September 21

And many false prophets will arise and lead many astray.

Matthew 24:11

🙠🙡

My voice is clear and strong. I call out to My sheep and they heed My voice. They do not go with those whose voices they do not know.

There are many voices in the world. False prophets clamor for the attention of both the goats and My sheep. Their words seem as a melody to the unsuspecting. They tickle the ears with promises of an easier way. They spew lies filled with worldly philosophies. They claim that compromise is the way and persecution is unnecessary. Many rush to travel this broad road. These fail to see the lies. What seems to lead to ease and safety from persecution actually leads to destruction—both in this life and the next.

You know My voice. It called you out of darkness and into life. Listen for it in the midst of this noisy world. It will lead you along your path. It will encourage you on those difficult days. Other voices seek only your destruction in this life. Pay no attention to them.

SEPTEMBER 22

They will put you out of the synagogues.
Indeed, the hour is coming when whoever kills
you will think he is offering service to God.

John 16:2

❧

When people define Me on their terms, things become confused. When religion is preferred over relationship, demonic deception abounds. Soon, those who should be allies have become enemies.

Persecution does not come only from the world. It also comes from My own people. Many of them do not understand My deep call to discipleship. They have substituted the safety of their religious practices in place of a vibrant relationship with Me. But no one stands before Me with the members of their religious group on the day of judgment. Each stands alone and is judged according to what they have done with what they were given. So strengthen yourself when such persecution comes. Those who pursue you in anger and fear do so because your freedom in Me threatens everything they believe. Let My love and mercy abound toward these who have been misled.

Do not be disheartened when persecutions come from those in My Church. They do not understand your great love for Me. But I do. It brings Me great delight. So stand!

SEPTEMBER 23

*But before all this they will lay their hands on you
and persecute you, delivering you up to the
synagogues and prisons, and you will be brought
before kings and governors for my name's sake.*

Luke 21:12

❧

Those who oppose Me persecute those who follow Me. Their
aim is to eliminate My influence in the world. In fear and
hatred they attempt to silence My truth by subduing My
followers.

Wherever My truth threatens the ways of the world,
opposition arises. There is outrage and indignation over My
message. Personal attacks filled with mocking and ridicule
are hurled against My disciples for their way of life.
Intimidation and threats come, and even violence. In the
midst of it all, I am with My children. I use what is meant
for evil to accomplish My good and perfect plans.

I am by your side. Never doubt this is so. When evil rises
up against you for My sake, look for Me. I will help you
stand against the onslaught and fulfill My purposes for
your life.

September 24

This will be your opportunity to bear witness.

Luke 21:13

❧

The deep purposes of My plans dwell beneath the surface circumstances of life. The wise plumb the depths of their trials, seeking to recognize what I am doing and remain in step with Me.

Those who persecute My children believe they are doing a great service for mankind. These assume their particular cause to be the beneficiary of their actions. But they are mistaken. They do not know My plans. They think they are pulling the plant out by the roots, but they are actually causing its seeds to drop into the soil of many hearts. In that day, these acts of evil will be turned to My glory by the words and demeanor of My disciples. Their witness will stand long after the cruelty has ended.

Look for Me in the day of your trouble. Seek out My intent in the matter. Do not allow circumstances to rule your day. Instead, let Me speak through you, planting seeds in the hearts of those around you. You will rejoice when you share in the harvest.

September 25

*And you also will bear witness, because you
have been with me from the beginning.*

John 15:27

❧

The Holy Spirit bears witness of Me in this dark world. He illuminates the words of My disciples, shining the light of truth in the hearts of mankind so they might see the error of their ways and turn to Me.

My disciples know Me. They have walked many miles by My side, learning My words and My ways. Because of this, their witness is strong in the truth of who I am and what I do. Each of My children is given the opportunity to share their testimony when they stand before those who oppose Me and oppress My people. The seeds of this testimony are sowed in the hearts of all who hear.

Your witness for Me stands tall in the world, whether good or bad. People watch to see if the words proclaimed from your lips match the attitudes of your heart and the steps of your walk. *When they look at you, what do they see?*

September 26

Settle it therefore in your minds not to meditate beforehand how to answer, for I will give you a mouth and wisdom, which none of your adversaries will be able to withstand or contradict.

Luke 21:14-15

༝ஜ༝

I flow freely through hearts yielded to Me. The owners of such hearts do not get in My way but follow as I lead.

I work in the moment whenever I can. I lead. I speak. I act. Those who follow Me closely have learned to allow Me to have My way in their lives. These tap into My power for their actions, My wisdom for their words, and My love for their attitudes. Those who encounter one of My children who are yielded to Me in this way are amazed. They hear but have no answer. Their arguments are overwhelmed by My truth. I cut deep into their hearts to expose their wicked ways.

Learn to quickly respond to My leading in your life. As we walk along the way, I will give you ample opportunities to do so. Then, in the day of adversity, I will speak through you to confound the proud and boastful.

September 27

*Do not be afraid, but go on speaking and do not be silent,
for I am with you, and no one will attack you to harm
you, for I have many in this city who are my people.*

Acts 18:9-10

૪৽৹

Persecution is a purifying fire. Opposition is a winnowing
fan. I am with those who stand in the midst of both and are
not scattered in the wind or consumed by the fire.

Where persecutions are, loud voices of danger and fear
cry out. These are like lions that paralyze the weak with the
fierceness of their roar. As opposition mounts, whispers of
safety and compromise abound. These are like serpents
who lull the unsuspecting by the subtlety of their ways.
Circumstances are not always as they first appear. I have a
remnant I can call forward in support of My plans at any
time. My children need only to listen to My voice and walk
forward as I direct. They will find that I have gone before
them to prepare the way. Others will appear and lend their
support.

In the midst of the battle, listen for My voice. It is not the
roar of fear or the whisper of compromise. It is the voice of
your Shepherd, the One who created you and called you out
from the world. Walk with confidence in the midst of your
enemies. You are not alone!

SEPTEMBER 28

*The one who hears you hears me, and the
one who rejects you rejects me, and the one
who rejects me rejects him who sent me.*

Luke 10:16

৵৵

You are not disregarded alone. You are not rejected alone.
You are not persecuted alone. I am with you in all these,
and My Father is with you as well.

You are of a different spirit than those of the world. I am
alive in you, and they are dead in their sins. You follow the
Living One, and they follow the god of their appetites. You
glory in My righteousness, and they glory in their
unrighteousness. You set your mind on heavenly things,
and they focus on earthly things. You are bound for an
eternity with Me, and they are destined for eternal
destruction. Walk, therefore, steps worthy of your high
calling. Do not return their deeds with like deeds of
disrespect, rejection, or hatred. You were once like them.
Stop and consider this with humility.

You have the Holy Spirit living in you. You are not the
same as you once were. Instead of being against Me, you
are now for Me. Instead of being on your own, you are now
with Me. Let your joy be full! Allow My love to lead you with
mercy toward those who hate you for My name's sake.

September 29

But I say to you who hear, Love your enemies,
do good to those who hate you, bless those who
curse you, pray for those who abuse you.

Luke 6:27-28

❧

Those who persecute you are blind. They do not know why they are doing what they do. They are driven by a hatred that is shared among all who do not know Me.

The passions of a fleshly heart want to retaliate in kind. Insults and anger, bullying and abuse, violence and hurt— these are the tools of those who torment My children. Though base and of the flesh, these are fueled by hate in the spiritual realm. I call My followers to bring their grievances before Me. I ask them to give their tormentors over to Me in prayer. I will deal with them. Only I can change a heart, turning it from its evil inclinations to what is good.

Do your part toward your enemies in the physical realm, and allow Me to do My part in the spiritual realm. Together, we will achieve the best result. Along the way, My love will grow in your heart, and you will become more like Me.

SEPTEMBER 30

I have said these things to you, that in me you may
have peace. In the world you will have tribulation.
But take heart; I have overcome the world.

John 16:33

᷈᷈

Each of My followers lives in two spheres of life. There is the world, and there is Me. These are opposed to each other. Where they meet, conflict occurs.

I have warned all who will follow Me of the tribulations they will experience in the world. I do not want any of My children to be deceived and think they can truly make friends with this world. For even the most wayward of My children will not find peace here but at best an uneasy truce. True peace is found in Me. It is the confidence of knowing that I understand what it means to be human. It is the assurance that I can uphold any who grasp tightly to My hand. It is the comfort of My love holding one close. I have overcome the world and all of its persecutions. I have conquered its trials and tribulations. I have trampled the enemy underfoot.

Take My hand in confidence. There is no trial too great, persecution too intense, or tribulation too deep that together we cannot overcome. This is My promise to you, My beloved. A promise of peace.

OCTOBER

Jesus taught that the heart was the determining factor of each person's walk with Him. He did not spare His words when it came to dealing with a hypocritical or judgmental heart.

OCTOBER 1

*Judge not, that you be not judged. For with the
judgment you pronounce you will be judged, and
with the measure you use it will be measured to you.*

Matthew 7:1-2

❧☙

I will judge every hypocrite. I will turn their critical
standards back upon them. Where no mercy was exercised,
none will be extended.

A critical, condemning spirit lacks mercy. I do not like
this in My children. Many rush to judgment based on
prejudices, biases, and opinions. They pound the gavel in
condemnation, never realizing they are revealing the evil
thoughts of their hearts and condemning themselves in
their pridefulness. Instead of looking upon others with an
arrogant attitude, I call My disciples to meekness and
humility. I want them to remember their own faults. Then,
they can judge with the same mercy I have shown to them
in the past. Where mercy is, love is not far away.

My child, I know it is easy to pass quick and harsh
judgment on the words and actions—and even motives—of
others. But this is not what I want to find in your heart.
Instead of such hypocrisy, recognize the urge to judge, and
then search your heart for the motive behind the urge.
What will you find?

OCTOBER 2

Why do you see the speck that is in your brother's eye, but do not notice the log that is in your own eye? Or how can you say to your brother, 'Let me take the speck out of your eye,' when there is the log in your own eye? You hypocrite, first take the log out of your own eye, and then you will see clearly to take the speck out of your brother's eye.

Matthew 7:3-5

❧❧

I do not excuse sin in the lives of My children. I bring it to their attention by the Holy Spirit so they can repent and move on from it.

It is easy to see sin in the lives of others. It is more difficult to admit the very same sin—or worse—in one's own life. The self-righteous point to others in judgment. They willfully remain blind to their own shortcomings. Sinful habits numb those who practice them. Ignoring the promptings of the Holy Spirit sears the conscience and burdens the heart. Soon, double-mindedness becomes a way of life. The outside of the cup looks clean, but the inside is filled with unrighteousness.

Maintain a clean conscience. Examine your life each day before the Holy Spirit. This will keep you far from self-righteousness and every arrogant attitude of superiority. *Even now, let us sit quietly together and see what is in your heart today that must change.*

OCTOBER 3

Let him who is without sin among you
be the first to throw a stone at her.

John 8:7

తలల

Everyone has sinned and fallen short of My glory. Not a day passes without a transgression against the holy God of all creation.

My Church has become indignant of the sin in the cultures around them. All manner of judgmental attitudes and words have found a home with My people. Many who shake their heads and point their fingers cannot see the hypocrisy of their actions. They are quick to pick up stones to throw even as they are overcome by their own sins. The world sees this and accuses them rightly of duplicity. Their witness is tarnished, and their impact is brought to nothing.

You have been forgiven of much. Yet, each day you sin. Remember, the world has not been redeemed. It does not walk in My new nature. Drop your stones and attend to your own repentance. You can then be a light in the dark world and a great witness through the power of a changed life.

OCTOBER 4

Pay attention to yourselves! If your brother sins, rebuke him, and if he repents, forgive him, and if he sins against you seven times in the day, and turns to you seven times, saying, 'I repent,' you must forgive him.

Luke 17:3-4

❧

I am the God of forgiveness. I keep forgiving even while I am exhorting My children to cease their sinning against Me.

The marks of self-righteousness are many. Prideful hearts and arrogant attitudes top the list. Where these are found, unforgiveness is sure to be near. How is it that My children can refuse to forgive those who have wronged them? Have they forgotten that I forgive them each time they come to Me with a repentant heart? Remember that your sins against Me are many. Then, when someone comes to you and humbly seeks your forgiveness, you can grant it with the great joy of one who has been forgiven much themselves. This is the way of My disciples.

While your sin grieves Me, granting you forgiveness brings Me great joy. In it, I see that you have turned away from your sin and back to Me. Go and do likewise for those who have offended you. Do it from a heart of gladness because someone has been restored.

OCTOBER 5

*Do not give dogs what is holy, and do not throw
your pearls before pigs, lest they trample them
underfoot and turn to attack you.*

Matthew 7:6

ﾏﾏﾏ

My truth is made alive by the Holy Spirit. My words, spoken to the secret places of the heart, accomplish what I intend.

My children engage in endless struggles against those who are in the world. They argue vehemently in My name while quoting My words. Their indignation exceeds their love. Their anger exceeds their mercy. What do they expect to accomplish with angry squabbles? How can truth be delivered to an unregenerate heart with daggers of hate? Is this not foolishness? Will it not cause the subject of their ire to turn against them with resentment and hostility? Instead, I call My children to avoid foolish quarrels. I ask them to speak the truth with My love. Self-righteousness avails little. The Holy Spirit can accomplish much. *Let the wise hear what I am saying to them.*

Do not quarrel with others, whether in My Church or in the world. If their hearts are hardened, they will refuse to hear. Instead, salt your conversations with patient endurance. Ask Me to work, and then see what I will do through the power of the Holy Spirit. We will rejoice together over those who have received My truth.

OCTOBER 6

Do not judge by appearances, but judge with right judgment.

John 7:24

❧

I judge according to the truth of the matter. I see the intents and purposes without bias or prejudice.

Some make it a practice to judge by appearance. Their hearts condemn by impressions and perceptions. Others judge according to their biases. Their hearts refuse to be swayed by contrary facts. Some judge by their wills. Their hearts will not engage beyond their settled ideas of what is right or wrong. Others judge from their hypocrisy. Their hearts cannot reconcile that their own actions are similar to those they scorn. Right judgment is based on truth, not opinion. It looks at the facts, not the preconceptions. It is faithful and without motives. It deals in mercy and not malice. It loves and does not despise.

Do not rush to judgment. Things are not always as they seem. Keep your heart pure and free from preconceptions. Listen for My voice. I know what is truthful and right. I will tell you what I see, both in your heart and with the matter at hand.

OCTOBER 7

I can do nothing on my own. As I hear, I judge,
and my judgment is just, because I seek not my
own will but the will of him who sent me.

John 5:30

❧❧

I judge all matters rightly. My children can do the same. All they must do is to stop and ask Me. I then show them what is right and what is true.

Human logic defies right judgment. It is low and fleshly, full of subtleties and nuances. It is easily swayed by the biases and preconceptions of the heart. The resulting blind spots lead to hypocrisy in action. Godly wisdom is right and true. It flows from My heart to the hearts of those who seek it. All I require of My children is that they humbly ask it of Me. Those who wait for My answer will gain My perspective. They can then interpret the matter and judge justly.

My child, you cannot hope to gain a proper interpretation of events without My input. Seek My will, and gain My perspective. You can then become wise in My ways, and your judgment in matters will be just.

OCTOBER 8

*You are those who justify yourselves before men,
but God knows your hearts. For what is exalted
among men is an abomination in the sight of God.*

Luke 16:15

❧

I see into the heart of every human. I discern its preferences and its intent. Though a person is justified and admired by their associates, I call out their wickedness and hypocrisy.

Every hypocrite is right in their own eyes. The sin of pride blinds their hearts to the truth. They seek out others who share the same opinions, finding justification in numbers. When called to account, these same ones protest their innocence and declare the purity of their motives. Though they fool many with their deceptive works and loud proclamations of fidelity to the truth, inwardly the evilness of their hearts cries out to Me. I condemn them and all who share in their hypocrisy because I clearly see their intent.

Do not be like the hypocrites. I have called you to a more perfect purpose than this. Let your actions come from pure motives. Seek to be pleasing to Me—the one who judges the rightness of your heart—and not to those who applaud you and tell you what you want to hear.

OCTOBER 9

*Beware of practicing your righteousness before other
people in order to be seen by them, for then you will
have no reward from your Father who is in heaven.*

Matthew 6:1

❧

Every act is judged for its motive and every word for its
attitude. Those done from a pure heart for My glory are
rewarded in heaven. Those done for personal benefit are
rewarded on earth by the fickle praise of mankind.

Righteous acts done with wrong motives are not
righteous but self-serving. This is a grievous sin among My
people. Whether doing good works out of a sense of duty, or
throwing My name around as a mark of holiness, or
performing conspicuous acts of devotion to be noticed,
these display the common thread of wrong motivations.
Instead, I look for acts of service and devotion from My
children motivated only by their love for Me. The more
unpretentious the act, the higher My regard and the greater
the eternal reward.

I know you because I created you. I understand your
personality and your preferences. My love for you is pure.
My devotion is perfect. *Why do you do what you are doing
for Me?*

OCTOBER 10

Those who are well have no need of a physician,
but those who are sick. Go and learn what this
means: 'I desire mercy, and not sacrifice.' For I
came not to call the righteous, but sinners.

Matthew 9:12-13

இ‐ை

I set the self-righteous aside. I cannot use them in My
kingdom. They live in bubbles of imperfect holiness,
keeping their hands from the dirty business of meaningful
engagement with those who need a touch of My love.

I work one heart at a time. Those who love Me do as well.
These have learned the true meaning of *mercy*. Sacrifice for
many is merely a good religious act performed in My name.
It is sterile and compartmentalized—a box to be checked off
on a list of righteous duties. There is no obligation beyond
the act to make an investment of the heart. Mercy, however,
requires more. The heart must become engaged in the
action. Compassion, listening, laughing, crying, and loving
follow an invested heart. These become My helping hands
in a hurting world.

Give Me your heart. I will place My great mercy into it.
You can then spread this mercy to those in need. I promise
that you will never be the same. You will be more like Me.

OCTOBER 11

Therefore I tell you, her sins, which are many, are forgiven—
for she loved much. But he who is forgiven little, loves little.

Luke 7:47

❧

The self-righteous have little need of forgiveness. For this
reason, their hearts hold little love for Me.

My salvation reaches out to the ends of the earth. It is
given to those who will answer My call. I save sinners great
and small. No matter how deep or how dark, I cover their
sins with the blood of My sacrifice. Some of My children
refuse to remember who they once were. These deny the
truth of their past lives, fearing for their standing in the
eyes of others. In their denial, they lose the keenness of
what I have done for them. Their love for Me lacks the
vibrancy of gratitude. With works they seek to fill the void
that their love for Me should occupy. Others, though,
remember the shame of bringing their helpless lives before
My cross. These know who they would be without My
graciousness. In humbleness, they thank Me for the
greatness of their salvation—a greatness matched by their
love and devotion to Me.

Your salvation cost My very life. Do not brush it aside!
Remember with Me, and celebrate My great love for you and
mercy on your behalf. Let the love of your gratitude flow
freely from a heart that has been set free.

OCTOBER 12

*Now you Pharisees cleanse the outside of the cup and of the
dish, but inside you are full of greed and wickedness.*

Luke 11:39

❧❧

I created man, inside and out. I look for the inside to be
cleansed, knowing the outside will follow. The self-righteous
do not see it this way. They polish the outside for the world
to see while the inside remains defiled.

I seek to cleanse the hearts of My children. This process
begins at salvation and continues for the rest of their
earthly lives. Such cleansing requires great humility on the
part of My followers. I look at each area of their lives. Those
places I find unpleasing are brought to their attention in My
timing by the convicting work of the Holy Spirit. By each
person's permission, work is done in the deep recesses of
their heart. Years of accumulated darkness are dredged out
and newness of life is poured in. Some, however, resist the
process of sanctification. These deflect every attempt to
plumb the depths of their hearts. Instead, they exert
themselves to maintain the outward appearance of their
lives, keeping all the sins and hurts hidden on the inside.

I long to heal you from the inside out. Yield your heart to
the working of the Holy Spirit. Release your secret sins and
painful wounds. I can heal them if you will only allow Me to
do so. You can experience freedom that comes with being
clean on the inside.

OCTOBER 13

*You hypocrites! Well did Isaiah prophesy of you, when
he said: 'This people honors me with their lips, but
their heart is far from me; in vain do they worship me,
teaching as doctrines the commandments of men.'*

Matthew 15:7-9

❧

My ways are perfect. There is no need for twisting or
turning. My ways are simple. There is no need for
enhancement.

I came to set My children free. This freedom begins with
a rescue from the slavery of sin and its pronouncement of
death. It progresses to an escape from the bondage of
manmade rules and requirements. It ends with a walk
through the world with Me—one that is not limited by
human preconceptions but by My perfect will for each
disciple. Some people, however, have different ideas. They
seek to complicate My ways and shackle My children once
again. But in all of their scheming and deception, their
hearts have wandered far from Me. They have gone the way
of Cain, and their worship is nothing more than vanity.

By My blood, you have been set free to walk on your own
unique journey with Me. Do not become entangled with
those who want to control your walk or use it for personal
gain. Listen carefully to Me, and I will keep you from the
path of error leading back to bondage.

OCTOBER 14

*I know your works. You have the reputation
of being alive, but you are dead.*

Revelation 3:1

❧

I am not the God of the dead but the God of the living. I came to bring life. Those who abide in Me have this life. It is lived by the Holy Spirit and not by the flesh.

Many in My Church act as though they are alive for a few hours each week. They put on their masks, pick up My Word, and gather with My flock. To all who see them, they exude the vibrancy of a life lived in Me. But no life is found in them, only decay. They quickly return to the deadness of their ways in the private places of their lives. These have left their first love but proclaim they have not. They act like they are with Me, but they have fallen away. They are now pretenders.

Remain in Me and enjoy the abundance of My life. This is My desire for you. You will not have to pretend. My life will shine forth from you for all to see.

OCTOBER 15

Beware of the leaven of the Pharisees, which is hypocrisy.

Luke 12:1

৵৵

Hypocrisy has spread throughout My Church. Double-mindedness abounds with practiced deception. I am used for gain, and My words are twisted for profit. Those who do this protest their innocence. But they are as cunning as Satan was in the Garden.

There are many Pharisees in My Church today. These stand in front of My people, leaning upon their scholarly degrees or fleshly anointings. They arrogantly proclaim the rightness of their ways as they boast of their holiness, special titles, or secret knowledge. But these speak of their ways instead of teaching My truths. They covet celebrity status and reject humbleness. They take widows' mites and spend them on luxuries. They pridefully boast of their accomplishments, not Mine. They tickle ears with fleshly tales of riches and dominion and every spiritual abomination. Those who hear are willingly led to the slaughter. They are ignorant of My ways and do not know My truths. They have eaten bread laced with the leaven of the world. It seems delicious today but will turn sour in their stomachs soon enough.

Put on the eyes of spiritual discernment. Listen for My voice calling out to you. Do not partake of the evil leaven that can quickly corrupt your life. Instead, humbly learn My truth without bias. It will keep you safe in these perilous times.

OCTOBER 16

Nothing is covered up that will not be revealed,
or hidden that will not be known.

Luke 12:2

❧

Many practice corrupt ways in secret, but My children have My special attention. I see what they do, and I hear what they say. I bring their words, actions, and attitudes out into the open to praise or to reproach in My timing.

Justice demands a day of revealing. It calls for an account to be given for every thought, word, and deed. Those who follow Me in truth and practice righteousness will be honored on that day. Those who counterfeit My truth or holiness will suffer sorrow when their deceptive ways are made known. Their reproach will exceed anything they have gained by their wicked ways. *Let the wise hear the truth of My words.*

I patiently suffer the falseness of My children for a season. I then deal with them when the time for action has come. Do not be numbered with the foolish who think I will continue to overlook their willfulness. Repent from every corrupt way and walk in My truth!

OCTOBER 17

The scribes and the Pharisees sit on Moses' seat, so do and observe whatever they tell you, but not the works they do. For they preach, but do not practice.

Matthew 23:2-3

૭∾૬

I am the God of integrity. There are no deceptive shadows with Me. Those who stand and speak for Me must rightly handle My words of truth and then walk circumspectly in them.

The truths of My Word are to be understood and followed. Hypocritical teachers are to be understood but not followed. These walk on the path of their own making. Though they may teach in truth, their lives lack integrity. They say but do not do. They cannot be trusted in the critical moment. They have forgotten that they answer to Me—that I hold all who teach My children to a higher standard of judgment. I examine their words for truth and their actions for integrity. Woe to those who teach one thing but do another!

Live your life with integrity. Let your actions match your words. Then your words will be of consequence and your life full of meaning. If you need help with this, come and sit with Me. I will show you the way of truth and help you to walk into it.

OCTOBER 18

*They tie up heavy burdens, hard to bear, and lay
them on people's shoulders, but they themselves
are not willing to move them with their finger.*

Matthew 23:4

ॐ✦

My yoke is easy and My burden is light. Those who make it
so are true, and those who do not are false.

There are those who stand over My children with the
whip of condemnation. These drive My sheep along under
heavy burdens of rules, traditions, or dogmas. When My
followers stagger under a load they were never meant to
carry, threats of damnation or excommunication rain down
upon them. Yet, the taskmasters themselves do not carry
such a load. Neither will they stoop to take some of the
burden away. Instead, they are forever inventing more
requirements for those in their charge to carry. This is the
drudgery of religion. It makes hypocrisy of My easy yoke.

Be careful when choosing your taskmaster. Instead of a
human definition of what is right and proper, choose Mine.
It is the perfect load because I share it with you.

OCTOBER 19

They do all their deeds to be seen by others. For
they make their phylacteries broad and their fringes
long, and they love the place of honor at feasts and
the best seats in the synagogues and greetings in
the marketplaces and being called rabbi by others.

Matthew 23:5-7

❧

The religious displays of man do not impress Me. Instead of
outward adornment, I look at the inward intentions of the
heart. I see if they are for good or for evil.

Many congregate with My children in vain. Whether at
worship services or related gatherings, these seek to make a
show of their righteousness. They parade their adornments
before those in attendance, all the while looking for human
praise. Others use their religious positions as opportunities
to be given special favor or honor. These, likewise, seek the
praise of others. All of this is foolishness. My disciples know
My call to humility. They understand clearly that the
greatest among them is to be a servant of all. The
hypocrites, though, have forgotten My words. Soon those
who have been first will be last for all eternity, and those
who demanded service on earth will be required to serve in
heaven.

Do not worry what others may think, but seek My
approval. I will lift you up and celebrate your great love and
devotion for Me. Some will receive all of their rewards here
on earth in the form of human devotion. I have called you to
a better way. Walk with Me, and receive rewards in heaven
that never pass away.

OCTOBER 20

Woe to you, scribes and Pharisees, hypocrites! For you travel across sea and land to make a single proselyte, and when he becomes a proselyte, you make him twice as much a child of hell as yourselves.

Matthew 23:15

৵৵৽

I gather to Myself children for My heavenly kingdom. Others gather to themselves followers for their earthly kingdoms.

Many leaders in My Church have fallen prey to the numbers game—membership counts, weekly offering amounts, annual baptism rates, attendance figures, and budgets. By these, they gauge their success. But they are mistaken. My work on earth cannot be quantified in business terms. Local church membership numbers are not a measure of kingdom effectiveness. Baptisms are not a measure of discipleship. Offering amounts mean nothing at all. I look for the number of hearts I truly own. I measure the depth of devotion to Me. Local churches are filled with many who want little to do with Me. My kingdom is filled with those who love Me and are called to My purpose. The numbers game builds man's kingdoms by man's methods with man's followers. I build the kingdom of heaven with My children.

I have called you to be My child, not a number. Your value is greater than a checkmark on someone's scorecard. Your primary concern is to walk with Me. I place you where I will to accomplish My work for the kingdom. You must only be willing and ready to go and do all I ask of you.

OCTOBER 21

Woe to you, scribes and Pharisees, hypocrites! For you tithe mint and dill and cumin, and have neglected the weightier matters of the law: justice and mercy and faithfulness. These you ought to have done, without neglecting the others. You blind guides, straining out a gnat and swallowing a camel!

Matthew 23:23-24

❧❧

In My kingdom, justice, mercy, and faithfulness outweigh a treasury of gold. Money in any form is lifeless. It dwells in the account of its owner. Justice, mercy, and faithfulness are alive. They dwell in the hearts of those who are Mine.

In many churches, money is the most important matter. Great efforts are expended to gather it in. All manner of manipulation is used to pry it from unwilling fingers. It is meticulously taken from people by way of false teachings. I tell you plainly, your money is not My priority! I want your heart! With it, I can do great miracles. Within it, I can grow love and mercy, faithfulness and justice. Hearts are the building blocks of My kingdom, and acts of love are its currency. When a heart belongs to Me, giving is an unselfish act of joy, not one of compulsion, guilt, or ulterior motives.

Bring Me your heart. If I have your heart, I have your will. You can then be of use in My kingdom. If you are Mine, so is your money. By way of your heart, I gain access to it and know you will give it cheerfully.

OCTOBER 22

Woe to you, scribes and Pharisees, hypocrites! For you are like whitewashed tombs, which outwardly appear beautiful, but within are full of dead people's bones and all uncleanness. So you also outwardly appear righteous to others, but within you are full of hypocrisy and lawlessness.

Matthew 23:27-28

❧

Whitewash may look inviting, but it covers much sin and uncleanness. Those who employ its use know what foulness lies within. The unaware are drawn to it.

Who seeks the cover of whitewash? Is it not those who are covering personal tombs of deadness and decay in a display of hypocrisy? Whitewash is not an appropriate cover for those of My kingdom. My blood is the true covering. It signifies that what lies beneath has been made alive and new. This is the covering for all who will enter My kingdom.

Stay away from whitewashed tombs. Only the dead dwell there. Their odor is foul and their corruption is sure. Come close to Me. Breathe in My life. It is a sweet-smelling aroma. The righteous are found there, alive and invigorated.

OCTOBER 23

The Sabbath was made for man, not man for the Sabbath.

Mark 2:27

৵৹

I am the Lord of the Sabbath. It is a privilege, not a duty, to draw close to Me and come into My presence. So come freely, without compulsion. See what I am doing for you and in you.

Though I have said clearly that My Sabbath was made for mankind, some will not accept this. All manner of traditions, rules, and practices have come to dominate what was meant to be a joyful time of rest and worship. Instead of coming to Me with a humble heart eager for fellowship, many come out of a sense of duty or social obligation. Instead of departing refreshed to walk in My ways, many run back to their sinful lives without another thought. Such practices are another form of hypocrisy. The Sabbath is an opportunity for all of My children to run into My arms. Those who would come should do it willingly and with holy intent.

Leave your worldly cares at My feet as you come into My presence. I will give you the rest found only in an eternal perspective. Soon, you will dwell with Me forever. The Sabbath is but a foretaste of that glorious day.

October 24

*No one tears a piece from a new garment and puts it
on an old garment. If he does, he will tear the new,
and the piece from the new will not match the old.*

Luke 5:36

❧

I came to show the true way to My Father. It is new and it is
fresh. It has no place with the old, for the old cannot bear
it.

It is not possible to attach Me superficially to a sinful life
and expect a good result. A casual association will not
change behaviors. Yet, many attempt to do this. These
proclaim My name and associate with My people, but they
refuse to cast off their old ways. They are hearers of My
Word but not doers. It is the same with some in My Church.
Though they have My new nature, they will not walk in it.
Though they now belong to Me, they will not do as I ask.
The newness of My truth cannot abide with their old
rebellion. Like a new patch on old cloth, it only makes
things worse. Instead, the old must be abandoned for the
new.

You belong to Me. Do not try to mix your old life with
your new nature. It will only cause you pain and sorrow.
Instead, put off the old and embrace the new. This is My
desire for you. It will bring Me great joy to see it fulfilled.

OCTOBER 25

*And no one puts new wine into old wineskins. If he
does, the new wine will burst the skins and it will
be spilled, and the skins will be destroyed. But
new wine must be put into fresh wineskins.*

Luke 5:37-38

❧❦

My truth is powerful. It is fresh. It permeates the heart and
expands in one's life. Those tied to the old and rigid ways
cannot contain it. They are destroyed by its very nature.

Many say they want more of Me. Yet, it is often these
very same ones who will not bear with My truth. They are
comfortable with their accepted versions of Me. They will
not countenance anything more. Who I actually am and
how I really operate are too much for them to bear. These
will not allow Me to do a fresh work in their hearts and
renew their minds with the truth. In this way, they are like
old wineskins that are unfit for My service. Those who truly
want more of Me accept Me as I am. They are like fresh
wineskins ready to be filled with My new wine.

You are Mine. I long to fill you with My truth. I long to
teach you My ways. Do not allow the stiffness of your old
beliefs to limit your usefulness. Let Me remake you as a
fresh wineskin. I will fill you completely.

OCTOBER 26

And no one after drinking old wine desires
new, for he says, 'The old is good.'

Luke 5:39

❧

I did not come to accommodate the old and worn out views or practices. I came to bring in the new, and with it, life.

Many of My people are set in their ways. They have fixed in their minds the nature and limit of truth. They are comfortable in their beliefs, even though they believe in vain and do not know the truth. I am not a partial truth but the entire truth. I cannot be contained by the thoughts of mere humans. I did not come so My children could lead shallow lives. I came to give them abundant life, free from the constraints of the narrow-minded. The old is comfortable but not good. All who dare to take Me at My word will declare that the new is better.

Do not get comfortable in your walk with Me. I am showing you more of Me than before. I am taking you places you have not dared to go. I am giving you new insights from My perfect and eternal perspective. The old is not good. I am. Taste of Me and see for yourself.

OCTOBER 27

You know how to interpret the appearance of the
sky, but you cannot interpret the signs of the times.

Matthew 16:3

❧❧

I am moving upon the earth. I am revealing Myself more
fully to those who walk closely with Me.

Many inside My Church are seeking after signs and
wonders. In their haste for a spiritual experience, they
chase after every form of deception the evil ones put before
them. In their hunger, they do not stop to see that what
they are doing makes a mockery of the very God they seek.
Their actions are self-focused and self-serving. Their
attitudes are fleshly and prideful. Though they can sense I
am moving in a fresh way among them, they are looking in
the wrong direction. It is time for these wayward ones to
seek Me for My sake and not their own. Then, they will find
Me.

Do not chase after experiences. They will lead you astray.
Chase after Me. Seek My truth above every notion you
might have. You will find Me in all of My fullness. You will
see I am enough.

OCTOBER 28

Is this not the reason you are wrong, because you know neither the Scriptures nor the power of God?

Mark 12:24

→←

I cannot be known by way of intellectual musings. I can only be known by a heart stirred by the Holy Spirit.

Many of My people believe they have a clear understanding of spiritual things. These have developed intellectual boxes tied with logical cords to hold their version of God. But in order to do this, they have had to discount many of My clear teachings. They look to the church fathers for guidance instead of to Me. They seek to know but do not listen closely to what the Holy Spirit is saying to them. Their brains are active, but their hearts are cold. I am not a stale God who has finished working and sat down to wait for the end to come. I live and move among My children. My power flows through those who follow closely after Me.

Do not put limits on Me. I have so much for you if you will only accept it. I am not finished working. I have called you to be My hands and feet and voice and heart. Through you, I will show My power in an unbelieving world.

October 29

And if the blind lead the blind, both will fall into a pit.

Matthew 15:14

༒

I am the God of clarity and purpose. I know where I am leading each of My children. Those who follow Me are kept safely on the path I have chosen for them.

Hypocrisy and deception move among My people like hidden wolves among sheep. Many are targeted for slaughter and led away unaware. These are victims of their own desires. They do not know My truths, so they chase after lies that appeal to their flesh. Those who lead them away do so with clear intent. They know how to manipulate emotions and deceive with clever words. They, themselves, are willfully blind but think they have the truth. They do not walk on My path as they profess but have fallen into the ditch beside it. Those who follow such ones become trapped in the mud of false teaching. Only My truth can pull them out of the pit and set them back on the path.

My precious child, learn what is true. This will keep you from what is false. As we walk along the path, many will cry out to you to come and walk with them. Do not go, but remain with Me. My Word will light the way, and My words will keep you close.

OCTOBER 30

I thank you, Father, Lord of heaven and earth, that you
have hidden these things from the wise and
understanding and revealed them to little children.

Matthew 11:25

࿊

I have chosen what seems foolish to confound the wise and what appears weak to bring the mighty to nothing. I lift up the humble and bring down the proud. All of this is done so there can be no doubt that I am the power flowing through those I use to accomplish My work.

The proud and arrogant are confounded by the simplicity of My truths. Their minds are worldly, and their gods are power and intellect. They look upon those through whom I have chosen to work and mock their insignificance. They listen to the truths coming from the mouths of My servants and reject them as being foolish. Such people do not understand Me or how I work. They will not accept My truths but prefer their own. Many profess to be the keepers of My ways but reject every attempt I make to show them more of Myself. They are hypocrites puffed up in pride.

I have chosen you for My special work in this world. Do not be dismayed when you are mocked and belittled by those in positions of power. Though they laugh at your lack of training or attainment from their man-made institutions, I will demonstrate My perfect truth and power at work in you.

OCTOBER 31

I still have many things to say to you,
but you cannot bear them now.

John 16:12

☙❧

I have not finished speaking, nor have I ceased to move among the many peoples of the earth. I give more to those who seek Me and take away from those who think they have enough.

My children have as much of Me as they want. There is no limit with Me. I am greater than anyone can comprehend. I did much more throughout history than what has been written down. The words in My books provide enough truth so I can be known. But those who seek Me will find more. They will walk with Me and learn My ways. They will know Me as I know them. Many will reject this. They do not want more of Me. It threatens their orderly worlds and challenges their shallow hearts. It is more than they can bear.

Come and sit at My feet. Open your heart to My truth. I will give to you as much as you will seek. Of Me, there is no end. It is with great pleasure that I make Myself known to you. My child, become My disciple and learn of My ways.

NOVEMBER

Jesus' words illuminate every aspect
of our lives. His truth is light to our
feet as we walk upon His path.

November 1

*But rise and stand upon your feet, for I have appeared
to you for this purpose, to appoint you as a servant
and witness to the things in which you have seen me
and to those in which I will appear to you.*

Acts 26:16

❧

I appoint and I direct. Those who belong to Me stand and
do the things I say. They witness to others about My great
power and glory at work in their lives. They tell of My love
and mercy.

Each of My children is appointed to serve Me as I see fit.
Only I know the plans I have for them. These plans are not
based on their desires but on My perfect will for their lives.
If they are willing, I can make My desires their desires. As
they decide to follow Me, I come to them and guide them
along the way. I make Myself intimately known to them so
they are sure of My will in all I ask. Many have a desire to
serve Me but only as they see fit. These reject My leading
and go the way of their own dreams and desires. They do
not see Me because they do not want to follow where I lead.

I have chosen you and appointed you as a servant in My
work on earth. It is My wish that you would agree to the
path I have chosen for you to walk. Once your heart is
proven to be true to Me, you will see Me. I will be your
constant companion along the way.

NOVEMBER 2

Truly, truly, I say to you, whoever believes in me will also do the works that I do; and greater works than these will he do, because I am going to the Father.

John 14:12

❧❧

I continue to work through My children. I use them to accomplish great works upon the earth.

Which is a greater miracle, a changed heart or a healed body? Many point to the absence of miracles in My Church as proof these have ceased. They claim the miraculous was only for a time long since past. In so doing, these very people look past the great miracles occurring all around them—changed hearts, pardoned sin, love for enemies. These are part of the *greater things* My children are involved in. Yet, I am the God of miracles. I heal the sick and I raise the dead. I give wisdom to those in need. But I do not entrust such power to everyone. Only those who have prepared and have proven their fidelity to Me will see these greater things flow through them to others. The unbelieving and unprepared will not.

I have much I can do through you once you have fully yielded to Me. My power awaits to flow through your hands as a sign to those who do not believe and a blessing to those who do. Allow Me to prepare you to wield such power. When you are ready, I will grant it.

NOVEMBER 3

It is more blessed to give than to receive.

Acts 20:35

᠀

I have given freely of Myself. My disciples do likewise. They put aside all greed and covetousness and learn to give with joy.

Some give out of a sense of duty. Others give out of compulsion. My children give out of a grateful heart. Duty and compulsion are poor motivators because only the mind is involved. But gratefulness is different. It involves the heart. Because the heart is involved, the will is conformed, and joy finds its place in the act. Those who receive are blessed, but those who give are doubly blessed. The giver has first been blessed by receiving, and they are blessed again when they give. I give many things to My children. I ask them to hold these loosely in their hands. In due time, I may require that they pass these things on to someone else. It is My wish for them to do so with a cheerful heart.

Learn to be a cheerful giver. Remember that you have first received, or you would not be able to give. Let Me guide your giving. I know who I want to bless through you. *Are you willing to let go of anything I have given you?*

NOVEMBER 4

*I do not ask for these only, but also for those who will believe
in me through their word, that they may all be one, just as
you, Father, are in me, and I in you, that they also may be in
us, so that the world may believe that you have sent me.*

John 17:20-21

☙❧

My Father is in Me, and I am in My Father. We share a
oneness with the Holy Spirit.

My disciples are to be known by their love for one
another. They are part of the same Body—My Church. Each
is under Me—the head. Working together, each part
supports the whole. When in balance, My Body has great
power and relevance in the world. But look at what has
happened. My Church has become fractured and broken.
One part works against the other. There is little oneness of
purpose. The unimportant gets in the way of the important.
The differences overpower any unifying bonds. Love is
lacking.

Love your brothers and sisters in My Body. Seek unity on
the common ground of salvation, and let Me take care of
the rest. Practice spreading My love and mercy in the world.
Those who see this will no longer laugh in derision. They
will know it is My perfect power working through imperfect
people who love Me.

NOVEMBER 5

*If you abide in my word, you are truly my disciples, and
you will know the truth, and the truth will set you free.*

John 8:31-32

ஓ‍ஓ

Only My truth can set one free. My disciples know this and
follow Me into all truth. The longer they abide in what I say
to them, the more freedom they experience in this life.

I came to set the captives free. Those who believe in Me
are set free from the sentence of death caused by their sin.
Then, each must decide to abide in My truth and learn My
ways. Many do not understand this. They follow Me when it
is convenient or when their life is filled with urgencies.
These do not experience all the freedom I have planned for
them because they will not embrace My truth. Those who
walk with Me each day learn My truth. These experience
freedom from demonic forces and sin, from biases and
prejudices, and from hatred and condemnation. My truth
works in their hearts, cleansing and sanctifying them.
These become My closest disciples—My special ones.

I have so much of My truth to give to you. If you will
receive it with a humble heart, you can be set free from
much in this life. Your shackles and weights will be
removed so you can dance in joy and delight before your
Savior. Abide in My words to you as we walk along the way!

NOVEMBER 6

The one who has bathed does not need to wash,
except for his feet, but is completely clean.

John 13:10

❧

Whoever I have set free is free indeed. They have been washed by My blood. They have been baptized into My Body by the Holy Spirit. They have been given gifts for the journey. They have been set aside for My service.

My children are washed on the day of salvation. This bath in My blood is an eternal covering for their sin. It cannot be lost or taken away. It is and always will be. Nevertheless, as My followers walk through the world, their feet become stained once again by sin. If not regularly cleansed through confession and repentance, sin accumulates, hindering their walk. That is why I ask each one to examine themselves and respond to the conviction of the Holy Spirit. In this way, they are made clean and do not become entangled in sin.

Do not grieve the Holy Spirit. Listen for His promptings. Spend time each day examining yourself to see if any fault can be found. Be quick to confess and turn from the sin you find. Then, you will walk with the light steps of the forgiven. *Even now, what is the Holy Spirit saying to you?*

NOVEMBER 7

*But seek first the kingdom of God and his righteousness,
and all these things will be added to you.*

Matthew 6:33

❧

Seeking My kingdom first is making Me your priority. It is
leaving all worldly thinking behind and placing yourself
willingly in My hand. It is waiting for Me to show you the
next step when you do not know what it will be. It is the
way of My disciples.

Many of My children have never learned to trust Me for
their daily needs. Though they would profess otherwise,
they grasp tightly to their fragile strings of safety and
control, making sure they have what they need. These are
prone to providing for themselves each day by doing what
they think is best. They plan and plot and toil on. This
becomes their priority in a life of security and
accumulation. Those who love Me open their hands. They
give over their self-sufficiency, seeking to know what I want
from their lives each day and giving what I ask. They walk
away from their means of support into Mine. I am their only
security in this life. When these say they love Me, I know
they mean it. I can do much with followers such as these.

Learn to live dangerously in My hand. Place your trust
fully in Me. Allow Me to direct your path and send you
where I will. Make Me your insurance policy and your
provider. Then you can truly say I am your priority.

NOVEMBER 8

Simon, I have something to say to you.

Luke 7:40

৵৵

I discipline those I love and correct every son or daughter I have. By this, My children are trained, and their behavior becomes pleasing to Me.

The humble in heart take My discipline without complaint. They listen when I point out their futile ways and take it all to heart. These want to become more like Me. They are willing to endure a time of discomfort to gain the wisdom of a lesson learned. The self-righteous are rebellious in My discipline. They blame others or circumstances for their sinfulness. They kick against the goads of My correction. They return My patient love with anger and bitterness. I tell you, the way for such children is more difficult than it needs to be. These do not understand how motivated I am by what is best for them or how long I will patiently wait for them to gain wisdom.

Do not return the love of My discipline with anger. Instead, eagerly learn the lesson so we can move on. I will discipline you because you are My child. The only question is what length I must go to turn you from your evil ways. Respond quickly, and let us walk on.

NOVEMBER 9

Now he is not God of the dead,
but of the living, for all live to him.

Luke 20:38

৵৽

I am the God of the living. Though My children would die physically, yet they will live on with Me eternally.

This physical life is not *the life*, nor is eternal life *the afterlife*. Though they understand this to be a fact, many of My children do not live this way each day. Life here seems urgent. There are comings and goings, family and friends, busyness and turmoil. But life on earth is very short. It is only a whisper of the wind. Life as I intended it to be begins after physical death. There, perfect peace and contented joy are the ways of all who dwell with Me. Rewards earned are not fleeting but are enjoyed forevermore. Preparing for eternal life *is* urgent. *All who hear should stop and ponder this.*

I am your God forever and ever. Your walk with Me in this life is preparation for the next. Learn of Me and My ways now so when you enter into My eternal rest, you will know Me well.

November 10

Pay attention to what you hear: with the measure you use, it will be measured to you, and still more will be added to you. For to the one who has, more will be given, and from the one who has not, even what he has will be taken away.

Mark 4:24-25

આરીજી

My truth is alive. Those who hear it and seek to understand will be given more of it. Those who disregard it will slowly lose the truth they have to confusion.

In My words, truth is found. And in truth, life is found. Truth does not respect opinions. It cannot be twisted. Truth is. It stands throughout eternity. Twistings, turnings, and opinions are not truth. They are error and deception. Those who diligently seek to know the truth with their whole hearts will find it. Those who seek to conform truth to their own beliefs or biases will not. I give liberally of My truth to those who want it as we walk along the way. I build precept upon precept as they are able to comprehend it and are willing to live it. Those who mishandle My truth become confused. In their foolishness they mix truth with lies and lose its purity.

Walk in My truth. Apply it to your life, and then seek more. I will show you its deep meaning. I will open the eyes of your understanding. By it, your heart will be strengthened and your steps illuminated.

NOVEMBER 11

A prophet is not without honor, except in his hometown
and among his relatives and in his own household.

Mark 6:4

⤙⤚

The familiarity of family and friends can breed contempt for
those who walk closely with Me. These cannot see past
what once was to what now is.

Those who are truly My disciples suffer much resistance
and animosity among those who knew them as they once
were. Such people react out of their past experiences, not
knowing the power of the changed life they now encounter.
Many times, these people seek to drag My children back to
the comfort of the past. In the hardness of their hearts, they
will not accept the truth of the present. Their spirits war
against Me. Such unbelief will not be rewarded. My power
will not be unleashed in their midst.

My child, you belong to Me, not to the past. Though it
may be hurtful, understand that the rejection you suffer is
because of Me living in you. You are not who you once were.
You are so much more!

NOVEMBER 12

See that you do not despise one of these little ones.
For I tell you that in heaven their angels always
see the face of my Father who is in heaven.

Matthew 18:10

❧

I set an angel over each person who is called to My salvation. These spiritual beings minister to them as directed by the very throne room of heaven.

Everyone who is called to My salvation has an angel assigned to them. These are selected and sent forth on the day of their human charge's birth. These angels have special access to the throne of My Father because those they watch over are precious to Him. Throughout the life of these called ones, their angels provide protection from the evil ones as I direct. These angels remain with their human charges until the day of physical death and then are released back to heaven to serve there. Some people make it a habit to venerate these heavenly beings, but this is not proper. I created them for My purposes. They go and do only as I say.

Angels are at work on your behalf even though you may not see them. Their power is supernatural, like the power of the evil ones sent to destroy you. I direct them according to My will for your benefit. Know that their nearness is an extension of My great love for you.

NOVEMBER 13

Martha, Martha, you are anxious and troubled about many things, but one thing is necessary. Mary has chosen the good portion, which will not be taken away from her.

Luke 10:41-42

❧

Those who love Me spend time with Me. They put aside the busyness of their lives so they can draw close to Me and learn My ways.

Many of My children confuse acts of service in My name with truly being close to Me. These endlessly toil away, thinking they are working for My kingdom. But how many have considered My plans for them? How many assume what they are doing is pleasing in My sight? How many have even stopped to sit quietly in My presence and seek My will for them this day? I am not the God of monotony, nor am I merely an observer in this life. I know the plans I have for each of My children. They may not be the same today as they were yesterday. My walk is fresh and vibrant. *Make sure you are in step with Me.*

Do not get into the rut of routine. It is not My way for you. I want you to walk in the vibrancy of life, not in the coma of conformity. Take time to sit and consider what *I* have planned for *you* each day. This will keep duty far from our relationship so it can live and breathe in freedom.

NOVEMBER 14

*Take care, and be on your guard against all
covetousness, for one's life does not consist in
the abundance of his possessions.*

Luke 12:15

❧

Do not lay up earthly treasures for yourself, but strive to
become rich in Me. The things of the world are perishing,
but I will be with you forever.

Covetousness is a base sin in this world. It is born from
the lust of the eyes and flesh. It is nourished by the
pridefulness of life. Many are caught in its trap, both in the
world and in My Church. People see what others have and
desire to have the same for themselves. They look and they
lust, they scheme and they plot. The desire to possess
drives their lives, but it is the want of human gain and not
a desire for Me. Many in My Church listen to those who say
that they should be rich in the things of the world. I tell you
plainly, those who promote such ideas are poor in the
things of God. By their words, the falseness of their hearts
is revealed. They will answer for every person they have
enticed with the sin of greed and for every covetous act they
have encouraged. *Let all who hear take note and beware!*

Do not worship the idol of material possessions or bow
before the god of riches. Where your treasure is, there your
heart will be found. Make Me your treasure! Grow rich in
My truth! Only then will your life become satisfying. Only
then will you be content.

NOVEMBER 15

What is impossible with man is possible with God.

Luke 18:27

ॐ∽

I am the God of every possibility. Though man is limited, I am not. My power flows out to the ends of the earth.

I am always at work. Though man has his plans, Mine are greater. While man struggles with his circumstances, I rise above them. With a single proclamation, I calm the wind and the waves. By My word, the barren womb brings forth life. With one command, the dead are raised and the sick are healed. It is difficult for many of My children to see past the approaching storm. They run before it, looking for a solution in their human reasoning. If they would only cry out and take My hand, I would walk them through all that is coming. I would carry their load and give them rest. The proud in heart do things their way. They are confident in their abilities. The humble know they are weak. They run to My arms, believing I will make a way for them.

Do not doubt what I can do. Instead, come and see what I will do. Do not look through the eyes of human understanding. See with the eyes of faith. This is the way of all who follow Me.

NOVEMBER 16

Put out into the deep and let down your nets for a catch.

Luke 5:4

࿇

I take great delight when My children obey Me. Though they cannot see what I am doing, their faith in Me produces obedience to My wishes, and this obedience produces results that are supernatural.

As My children walk with Me, I ask them to go out into the deep waters and do things that appear to be impossible. In such places the shore is far away, and the bottom is out of reach. Water stretches out in every direction, isolating the boat. Here, I am the only security against the dangers. As I did with Peter, I ask My followers to fully commit and let down *all* of their nets in faith, not just some of them. At times such as these, I am asking for complete obedience in faith, not solutions from My children. I already know they have attempted similar things before without result. I see all of the impediments to success. I want to show them I can produce results from even a measure of their faith and grow it for future events.

Attempt what I ask of you with great faith, and leave the results to Me. Let down all of your nets instead of a few. I can only fill what you have put out.

NOVEMBER 17

Take away the stone.

John 11:39

❧

I work in the physical world, but My power comes from the spiritual world. I long to release this power in the lives of My children.

Many of My followers are bound by the tangible world of the senses. They cannot see past their human experiences or believe beyond the limits their minds have set for what could be possible. Heavy stones of human reasoning separate them from supernatural miracles that await just beyond what they can see. These unbelieving ones do not understand their poverty. They have become comfortable living far below what I have for them. But those who heed My call to remove such stones take away the limits on how I can work in their lives. These see My power unleashed and are never the same.

I long to energize the dead places in your life. Take away the stones blocking My work. Let Me infuse you with My supernatural power. You will be amazed at what I can do in you when you remove the unbelief of human reasoning.

NOVEMBER 18

*Everyone then who hears these words of mine and
does them will be like a wise man who built his house
on the rock. And the rain fell, and the floods came,
and the winds blew and beat on that house, but it did
not fall, because it had been founded on the rock.*

Matthew 7:24-25

৵৽

Shallow foundations will not stand in the day of adversity.
As the winds blow and the waves crash, only those
foundations that go down to the rock will hold firm against
the storm.

Many of My children have built houses on the sand.
Their walk with Me is minimal and their commitment is
shallow. These have not invested in foundations that will
hold in the storm. They have not dug down deep into a
rock-solid relationship with Me. The wise know they must
make an investment to get to the rock. They understand
that effort is required in order to dig deep. They have
allowed Me to inspect along the way to prove their work to
be adequate. Because these have not quit during the trials
of building our relationship, their house will not fall in the
storm. *How deep is your foundation?*

Building a house is not enough. It takes a firm
foundation on the rock to make it stand. I long to build
strong faith into your life—faith that is deep and unyielding.
If you will work with Me on our relationship, you will not
fail in the day of adversity, and your house will stand
through every storm.

NOVEMBER 19

*But I have this against you, that you have
abandoned the love you had at first.*

Rev 2:4

⧂⧆

I am the Bridegroom. You are My bride. Do you love Me as
much as you did on the day of our betrothal, or has your
love for Me cooled?

There is much joy on the day of salvation. There are
pledges of fidelity and love. There is excitement for the
times ahead. There is confidence that the relationship will
grow as time is spent walking together on the path. There is
a commitment to drawing more closely together, becoming
one in heart and mind as the day of My return draws near.
But many of My children have not kept their pledge to Me.
They have allowed their love for Me to grow cold from
neglect. Some have chased after idols. Others have
committed adultery with the world. I shout for all of these
wayward ones to turn from their sinning and return to Me. I
long to be their foremost love. I stand on the path and wait.

Remember back to the day of your salvation. Recall the
feelings of love and gratitude you had for Me. Think of the
excitement you held for our walk together and the
determination you had to follow Me. I am full of zeal for
you. I am completely committed. *Has your commitment to
Me grown as I have invested in your life?*

November 20

Those whom I love, I reprove and
discipline, so be zealous and repent.

Rev 3:19

❧

I have great zeal for you. Because I love you, I want what is best for you. When you go astray, I bring your sin before you and correct your waywardness.

There are times with each of My children when I must admonish them. It is always My hope they will take My correction quickly and return to the path we travel upon. Sometimes, though, My children stand aloof with uncommitted hearts. These consider themselves to be rich in all things without a need for Me. Such ones do not know how wretched they are apart from Me. They are overcome by their blindness and are pitiful to behold. For these, I must use the rod of discipline to bring them back to Me. I am committed to each of My children. I go to great lengths to rescue them from their foolishness.

I love you too much to allow you to go astray. Do not stand aloof with a lukewarm heart. Run to Me when you have sinned. Repent of your foolishness. Take Me by the hand and begin walking with Me once again. This delights Me greatly.

November 21

*Behold, I stand at the door and knock. If anyone
hears my voice and opens the door, I will come
in to him and eat with him, and he with me.*

Rev 3:20

☙❧

I am ever asking, always seeking, and persistently
knocking. I request access to the heart. Those who open
theirs to Me enjoy My fellowship.

What could be better than God visiting with man? What
could be more satisfying than a meal shared with the
Almighty? Yet, many shut Me out of their hearts each day.
They selfishly go about, doing what they want. Their hearts
are cold and closed. Still, I pursue these as a shepherd does
a wayward sheep. I know the dangers lying in wait for those
children who run from Me. Even as the wolves are upon
them, I knock fervently on their hearts, seeking to be
brought back into their lives. Such is My love for each of My
children.

Do not run off on your own. You have little idea of the
danger. The evil ones lie in wait for you. They seek your
total destruction. Throw open the doorway to your heart!
Let Me come in. I will restore our fellowship. I will lead you
back to your path.

NOVEMBER 22

The spirit indeed is willing, but the flesh is weak.

Mark 14:38

❧

The flesh is weak. It is made from the dust of the earth. It is the battleground in every human.

Many have promised to be strong, yet have failed in the time of trial. Many have pledged their undying fidelity but have been led astray by lesser things. Many have determined a bold path, only to be sent in retreat. Such is the weakness of the flesh. Every one of My children should take note of these truths. The place of battle with the demonic forces is always the flesh. It is the weak link in a strong chain. It is the point of entry.

Do not think more highly of yourself than you ought. You can be brought low in a moment by your pride. Cry out to Me for protection. Stay close to Me as we walk. You are not as strong as you think you are.

NOVEMBER 23

My food is to do the will of him who
sent me and to accomplish his work.

John 4:34

❧

I have called each of My children to walk with Me to the very end. This is the most satisfying use of their brief life on earth.

Food nourishes. It satisfies. It sustains. Those who walk closely with Me would say that this is the nature of our walk together. My disciples live to do what I ask, emulating My ways in all things. This is their greatest joy. It brings unparalleled satisfaction in their lives. The world tries to usurp My place in the lives of My children. It offers promises of wealth and ease and peace. It lures with its base pleasures. It assures contentment with its ways. In all of these, it sets a trap for the flesh. But My children are to walk by the Holy Spirit and not the flesh. They are to keep their eyes on the prize of their high calling and not on the world around them.

I have planned a great journey with you. It will bring you satisfaction and contentment. Do not turn aside to the false offerings of the world. It never keeps its promises. Instead, remain with Me. I am faithful, and I am true. Walk with Me and you will see.

November 24

It is I; do not be afraid.

John 6:20

❦

My love for My children is complete. It drives away all fear.

Those who abide in Me, abide in My love. Because My love is perfect, it wants only what is best for each of My children. It goes before them and follows after them. They encounter only what I allow in their lives. For this reason, My followers can boldly enter any task I give them to do. They need not fear. There is no reason to second-guess. Though they may not be able to see the path before them clearly, yet they can be confident that I am with them and will show them the way forward. They are in My will, and I am completely responsible for them. They can rest in this.

Do not hesitate in fear when I have spoken. Go boldly forward into what I have commanded. I have gone before you to prepare the way. I follow behind you to sustain the effort. Great things are accomplished only through faith in Me. I am worthy of your trust. *Are you doing all I have asked?*

NOVEMBER 25

*...not that anyone has seen the Father except
he who is from God; he has seen the Father.*

John 6:46

❧❦

The Father's glory shines all around Him. Thunder and lightening emanate from His throne.

No human has ever seen the Father face to face but Me. Human eyes cannot behold Him, whether in the flesh or in a vision. Even John did not see Him when I showed him the mysteries of what is to come. He saw only My Father's glory. The Father is the essence of purity. Sinful man cannot approach His holiness. This is why He sent Me to you. You can see Me because I have come among you as God in the flesh. I will present you to My Father on the day you enter heaven. You will be clothed in My righteousness and bow before His throne.

My Father and I are one. As *God with you*, you have seen the Father through Me. Let this be enough for you until you enter into heaven. Then, you will behold Him face to face in My presence.

NOVEMBER 26

So there will be one flock, one shepherd.

John 10:16

ॐঔ

I gather My children from all over the world. I bring them into My flock where they live forevermore.

I have only one flock. Those who do not belong to this flock are goats. My flock has been splintered by their ignorance and arrogance. Many have twisted My truth. Others have added laws and requirements. Some have orchestrated grotesque doctrines of error. All who have done these things have abandoned the simple purity of My words. Confusion now abounds. Group upon group has formed, each claiming an exclusive right to My favor. My sheep run from one pasture to another in search of the best grass. The furor has allowed deception to creep in undetected. Many who claim to represent Me are not of My flock but are goats. I call to My sheep, inviting them back to My truth. Only there will they find rest.

Do not run to the next fad, experience, or celebrity. Stay with Me. I will lead you along the path of righteousness. I will keep you in My truth. I will protect you from the wolves.

November 27

*Just as it was in the days of Noah, so
will it be in the days of the Son of Man.*

Luke 17:26

❧

One day, I will be revealed to the entire world. Many will
stand in dismay without preparation or excuse.

Some in My Church believe they are essential to My
return. These boast that they must prepare the way with
revival or I cannot come back. This is arrogant and foolish.
They cannot bring about revival by their works. Only the
Holy Spirit can by His works. There is no 'way' to prepare,
just humble obedience as the kingdom is built one heart at
a time. There will not be a great revival before I come back
but a great falling away from My truth. People will be busy
with their lives up until the very end. They will be preparing
only for the next day, week, or year, not for My return. The
day of My coming will fall on them as suddenly as My
judgment fell on those in the days of Noah or Lot. And as it
was in those days, there will be no relief or reprieve for
those who have rejected Me.

My child, do not become caught up in preparing the
world for My return. Instead, prepare your heart. Do what I
lead you to do each day. Remain steadfast, not propelled
erratically by hype. My Father has a plan. You cannot
change it. So rest in the works I have for you to do, and
leave all else to Me.

November 28

*Go home to your friends and tell them how much the Lord
has done for you, and how he has had mercy on you.*

Mark 5:19

❧

My children overcome the enemy by My blood and the word
of their testimony. The first, I contribute. The latter, they
add.

Each of My children has a testimony. It is their
statement of a changed life. It begins before they know Me
and ends on the day of their death. A testimony is powerful
because it is not a story told by others but a first-hand
narrative of My work in a life. It stands as a witness to all
who hear it. A testimony is precious. It is to be guarded
against defilement. Many of My people have allowed the
world to rob them of the power of their testimony. These
walk with one foot on My path and one in the world. Theirs
is a tale the world likes to hear—one of compromise and
shallowness. But even with these, it is not too late. They
can overcome their falseness by running back to Me. Then,
their testimony will tell of the great power of My faithfulness
in the lives of even My wayward children.

As we walk together, you add to your testimony. It is the
great narrative of our life together. Endeavor to keep it
powerful by keeping it pure. I will use it in the lives of
others. By it, you will share in My harvest.

NOVEMBER 29

You are my friends if you do what I command you. No longer do I call you servants, for the servant does not know what his master is doing; but I have called you friends, for all that I have heard from my Father I have made known to you.

John 15:14-15

❧

My friends do what I tell them out of their love for Me. My servants do what they must out of their fear of Me.

It is My desire that each of My children would become My friend. For this to be possible, these must put My will above their own. They must do as I have commanded them to do. They must lay down their lives for Me as I have laid Mine down for them. Many of My children do not become My friends. These love themselves more than they love Me. Their only desire is to go their own way and live their lives for themselves. They must be compelled by fear or force to do what I have told them to do. Though these like to think of themselves as My friends, they are not. They are servants who share a servant's mindset.

I have reached out to you in love. I have shared My plans for your life. I am ready to share a relationship that is closer than any brother's. Now you must respond. *Are you a servant or a friend?*

NOVEMBER 30

Yet a little while and the world will see
me no more, but you will see me.

John 14:19

☙❧

The world cannot see Me. It sees only the evidence of My reality. I have granted the privilege of seeing Me to My disciples.

I did not leave My children as orphans. They have the Holy Spirit in them and Me at their side. Many believe I have left the earth, only to return in the future. These imagine Me to be seated at My Father's right hand, waiting for My turn to get involved with the world once again. But those who truly know Me know the truth. I walk with them each day. I talk with them and they with Me. For those who have proven their loyalty to Me, I am even more involved. These see Me.

It is with great pleasure that I appear to My children. I would like to share this privilege with you. Seek Me with your whole heart. Learn of My truths. Walk faithfully with Me, turning neither to the left or the right. When I judge that your fidelity to Me is sufficient, you will see Me.

DECEMBER

Jesus is Lord over all. Let everything that has breath praise Him. Let each of us bow down and worship Him.

DECEMBER 1

Truly, truly, I say to you, before Abraham was, I am.

John 8:58

❧

I have no beginning, and I have no end. I was and now am and will always be. I am.

I am inconceivable. I cannot be fully understood by the human mind. Who can grasp the mystery of the Trinity or the truths of election and choice? How can I exist as both man and God at the same time? How do foreknowledge and free will coexist? *I am uncontainable.* I am bigger than the box of any man's thinking. Who alone could speak creation into being? Who could design with such attention to detail? Who knows the ways of man even better than man himself? *I am undeniable.* Those with spiritual eyes can see Me at work all around them. Who can look at creation and not see My fingerprints? How can all people share a basic idea of what is right or wrong if everything came about by chance? How can those who know you explain your changed life other than by a miracle of God? Because I am, all of these can be also.

Be still and know that I am God. I am your Creator. I am your Redeemer. I am your protector. I am your friend. Walk with Me, My child. Marvel that you are in the very presence of the Almighty.

DECEMBER 2

All things have been handed over to me by my
Father, and no one knows who the Son is except the
Father, or who the Father is except the Son and
anyone to whom the Son chooses to reveal him.

Luke 10:22

જ્જ

I am the visible manifestation of the Godhead. I was sent to
be in the world with My children.

Though My children know Me, they have not seen Me in
all of My glory. Though they walk with Me along the way
and talk with Me, they have but a glimpse of all I am. My
Father knows all I am since He is in Me and I in Him. Those
who would know My Father must know Him through Me. I
reveal Him to those who seek Him through Me because I am
the only way to Him. As My children get to know Me, they
get to know My Father. As they experience Me, they
experience My Father through Me. I do nothing on My own
but only by His will. This is the same wish I have for My
children—that they would do nothing on their own but only
by My will.

In Me, you have access to My Father in heaven. Draw
near to Me so you can draw near to Him. Seek My will in all
things. When you do, you are seeking the very will of My
Father for your life.

DECEMBER 3

All authority in heaven and on earth has been given to me.

Matthew 28:18

⮟⮜

I am the Creator of all things. I hold the very atoms of the universe together in My powerful hands.

My Father has given Me all authority to execute His perfect will and plan. I work in His name as I have done since the beginning. My authority originates in heaven and extends throughout the created universe. There is nothing so small it can escape My notice. By My authority, My children are put to work for the kingdom. They do not go out on their own but by My word. Some do not understand this. They get out from under My authority and do what seems best to them. Even though they attach My name to their work, it does not belong to Me because I have not authorized it. *Let all who work for Me do so under My direction.*

It is My great pleasure to exercise My authority on your behalf. As you labor for the kingdom, this is the source of all power. Do not waste your life working without My power. Remain under My authority in all things.

DECEMBER 4

Which is easier, to say to the paralytic, 'Your sins are forgiven,' or to say, 'Rise, take up your bed and walk'? But that you may know that the Son of Man has authority on earth to forgive sins...I say to you, rise, pick up your bed, and go home.

Mark 2:9-11

ༀ

There are miracles of the heart and miracles of the flesh. Some are spiritual and others are physical. I have the authority over all of them.

Many think of miracles only in terms of healing or bringing the dead back to life. While I do work in the physical realm restoring health or vision, hearing or speech, limbs or even life, I do so much more. A changed heart is My greatest miracle. It is a spiritual miracle, impacting a life even more than a physical healing. It is an eternal miracle, lasting beyond the reaches of this life.

You belong to Me. You have already experienced the greatest miracle in your life. Never lose the wonder of how you were changed from what you once were into what you are becoming in Me.

DECEMBER 5

Peace! Be still!

Mark 4:39

༂

As the God of creation, all of nature responds to My commands. From the smallest microbe to the largest animal, from the slightest breeze to the hurricane, from a ripple in a pond to the waves of the sea, all must obey the sound of My voice.

Many do not understand how I work in the created universe. Some believe I set it in place and left it to function on its own. Others believe I command its every move. Both are right, and both are wrong. I am the sustaining force of the universe. I have also put systems and laws in place by which everything functions. Sin has disrupted the perfection of My creation, bringing with it destruction and death. Wills and choices play into the great mystery of life. Yet, I have the ultimate authority over all. Only by My permission are things allowed.

I intervene in your life for your ultimate good. I allow some situations to pass through to you and forbid others from coming near. Everything is done out of My great love for you. Each has a specific purpose in your life as I shape you into My image.

DECEMBER 6

I tell you, if these were silent, the very stones would cry out.

Luke 19:40

🙴

All of creation sings praises to its Creator and to His Father in heaven.

In the beginning, I created everything for the pleasure of My Father. In the perfection of its order and its function, creation shouted out its praise to Him. From the birds of the air to the fish in the sea, each called out in praise as it fulfilled its purpose in this world. The stars sang from the heavens and the waves roared from the sea. Even mankind joined in as I walked with them in the Garden. Creation now groans under the weight of sin as it awaits the day of its redemption. Yet, songs of praise ring out to heaven. The leaves on the trees clap their hands, and creatures call out. The sun bursts forth with light and warmth, while the moon declares its quiet peace. And then there are My children. They join with the rest of creation by lifting their hearts in praise to the One who created them.

I am worthy of your honor and praise. Do not keep silent. Let My joy well up in your heart and overflow. Sing out your praise to your God with a shout of thanksgiving! Alleluia!

DECEMBER 7

For this reason the Father loves me, because I lay down my life that I may take it up again. No one takes it from me, but I lay it down of my own accord. I have authority to lay it down, and I have authority to take it up again. This charge I have received from my Father.

John 10:17-18

❧

My love for My children is intentional. I laid My life down for them and took it back up again with purpose.

When My Father sent Me into the world as a baby, He did so with a specific plan in mind. He gave Me the authority to walk in that plan and do the works of His will. Day after day, I laid My life down for those around Me to show them the way to My Father. On the cross, I died to pay the redemption price for those who would come to My Father. When I rose up from the grave, I opened the door so these same ones could worship forever at My Father's throne. Everything was done for My Father—the laying down and the taking up of My life—so His plan for you would be complete. Through Me, He extended His love to you. Through Me, you have access to Him.

I showed you the greatest love of all when I died in your place. You will be seated with Me in heavenly places. You will sing the song of the redeemed. You will worship at the throne of your Father forever. Let Our love wash over you and fill your heart with joy!

DECEMBER 8

For the Son of Man is lord of the Sabbath.

Matthew 12:8

ജ∾ക

I created the Sabbath for My children. It is a day to rest and celebrate My great love for them.

I am the Lord of the Sabbath. On the seventh day of creation, I rested from My creative labors. I enjoyed what I had made, the work of My hands. I left this as an example for My children. It is My desire they would have a regular time of rest, enjoyment, and thanksgiving in My presence. Only I can say what My children will do on this day. For some, I will direct them to gather together for a time of instruction and worship. For others, I will take them away from every care to walk with Me in the solitude of My creation. Others, still, will be about My business on that day. I have done all of these things and more on the Sabbath—I taught, I listened, I worked, I spent time with those I loved, and I feasted. My children should seek the direction of the Lord of the Sabbath. I know what I have planned for each one on that day.

I made the Sabbath. It is Mine to give to you. I will have you celebrate it in many different ways according to the season of our walk together. If you follow Me in this, I will keep the Sabbath fresh and far from becoming a duty. Let us share these times together in joy, unshackled from the ways of man.

DECEMBER 9

Cast the net on the right side of the
boat, and you will find some.

John 21:6

૰ৡ

I find great joy in blessing My children. I wait for them to cease from their striving so I may do so.

Who would resist a blessing from Me? Many would declare that anyone who did was out of their mind. Yet, each of My children does this very thing from time to time because of their busyness. Sometimes, they get in the way of My blessing, blocking it by the efforts of their own hands. Other times, they get out in front of My blessing, working away on their own when I have not yet prepared the way. Many times, they miss My blessing altogether because they are not looking to be blessed. When My children stay in step with Me, they see how much I bless them. Sometimes, it is in a small thing. Other times, it is in a big way. In every case, each blessing I give points back to Me. It is an opportunity for praise.

Stay with Me as we walk. Remain attentive along the way. You never know when or how I will bless you. It may be through an act of kindness. It may be the flight of a butterfly. It may be the joyous laughter of a child. My blessings abound. *Are you receiving them?*

DECEMBER 10

Lazarus, come out.

John 11:43

❧

My commands are powerful, and they are specific. By them, mountains are moved and impossibilities are shattered.

If I would have simply cried, *Come out*, every grave on earth would have emptied. But I wanted only one grave to give up its dead, so I shouted to Lazarus alone. There are times when My commands are for all of My people. But most of the time, I give commands to specific individuals for singular tasks. In this way, I lead My great army on earth in general, while directing specific actions individually. The group should not judge My commands to the individual, nor should the individual judge the commands I give to the group. Instead, each follower should acknowledge My greater purposes and allow Me to lead as I please.

Much of the time, I will be directing you to a particular purpose in a specific way. Do not be concerned that others are not directed the same. Likewise, do not allow others to dissuade you from your task. Instead, know that this is My kingdom working at its best—many specialists on assignment, all belonging to the same group.

DECEMBER 11

*For as the Father raises the dead and gives them
life, so also the Son gives life to whom he will.*

John 5:21

ༀ

I give life to those who follow Me. First, it is eternal life.
Then, it is My abundant life. Blessed are those who have
both.

When I give My children eternal life, it is only the first
step on the journey with Me. It begins in this life and
continues endlessly in heaven. But on this side of heaven,
there is also an earthly life to be lived. Whether for a few
moments or for many years, it is a life lived in the world as
My child. Just as eternal life is abundant, so can this life be
for My children. Many never find it, though, because they
look for it in the things of the world. They forget I have
warned them that life is not about *accumulating* but
spending. As these give their lives away for My sake, they
make more room for Me. This is where true abundance is
found—in more of Me. Only I can satisfy the needs of My
children. Only a walk with Me can fulfill their destiny.

I have given you life. I want you to live it to the fullest in
Me. As you die to yourself, you will live more abundantly in
Me. As you spend your life for Me, you will gain more of Me.
Each day, less of the journey through this life remains.
With every step, you get closer to your destiny.

December 12

Heaven and earth will pass away,
but my words will not pass away.

Mark 13:31

☙◦❧

When all else fails, My truth remains. Whether written down or not, none of My words will fail. They are truth. Truth lasts forever.

My words are truth. Every one of them will stand, whether spoken in the past or in the future. I have had much to say in the past as I spoke to My people throughout the years. Some of it was captured in the pages of Scripture from Genesis to Revelation, but most of it was not. I have much to say to My children today and even more to say to them in the future. Only those who are listening can hear and be filled. The rest continue walking in poverty with their crumbs. Everything I say is consistent with what has been said before—both what was written down and what was merely heard. This is the essence of My truth. It is perfect. It can be no other way.

Do not fear that you will not hear Me correctly. I will never contradict what I have previously said. By this, you can be sure of My words to you. So listen for My voice. I have much to say to you.

December 13

Have you never read in the Scriptures: 'The stone that the builders rejected has become the cornerstone; this was the Lord's doing, and it is marvelous in our eyes'?

Matthew 21:42

❧

The kingdom of heaven is built upon Me. I am the cornerstone that makes the walls straight. Without Me, all would fall. This is marvelous, and it is true.

Many try to build their own kingdoms in this world. They formulate their own plans. They use their own materials. They apply their own labor. They make their own rules. They gather their own followers. Such kingdoms are built upon the sand. They will fail in the day of calamity. There are those in My Church who make the same mistake. They begin with their own plans and end with their own followers. These, too, build in vain on the sand. My kingdom is true. Its foundation is sure. I make its walls straight and solid. Many discard the most important stone in their building program. I am that stone. I make all of the difference.

Do not forget Me in all of your doing. Nothing of eternal value can be built if it is not based on Me. You have been given natural capabilities and supernatural gifts. Make Me your sure foundation while you use them for the kingdom.

DECEMBER 14

Do not think that I have come to abolish the Law or the Prophets; I have not come to abolish them but to fulfill them.

Matthew 5:17

❧

I came to do for you what you could not do for yourself. Only I could fulfill the Law and satisfy the Prophets. These had condemned you, but you are saved in Me.

Only those who repent of their evil deeds can put on My robe of righteousness and stand blamelessly before the Law. The Law, and the Prophets who upheld it, condemn all others. This is why My Law will stand until all is accomplished. It will continue to condemn those who do not know Me. This was always the purpose of the Law—to show that righteousness could not come from the performance of works and rites but only from God alone. The humble see this clearly, desperately throwing themselves upon My mercy and love. But the proud walk on, futilely hoping their works will be enough.

I have removed the penalty of the Law for you. I have brought you into a new covenant with Me. Works of righteousness could never satisfy the Law. It took My blood shed on your behalf. No other payment is necessary. You are now free in Me to do the works I have given you.

DECEMBER 15

I came to cast fire on the earth, and
would that it were already kindled!

Luke 12:49

☙❧

I brought the fire of purification to the world and kindled its flame. It is a fire wrought from My truth. This fire separates all people into two groups—those who accept My truth and those who do not. Now that it has been started, this fire must burn until the final day.

My fire is alive and burning throughout the earth. It separates truth from error, burning the chaff from every life. Many cry out to Me, asking Me to send fire down upon them. These do not know what they ask. My fire is already here. It is the fire of purification administered by the Holy Spirit. This fire rages with My truth, judging all who are in error. Without first undergoing this purification, no one will receive a full measure of My power. How greatly I desire that My Church would allow this fire to burn within and purify the hearts of all who are Mine!

The power of the Holy Spirit will purify you if you allow it. He will convict you of the error and falseness in your life. The more He can work, the closer together we will walk. Do not resist Him, but let Him have His way. *What is He pointing to right now in your life?*

DECEMBER 16

Whoever has seen me has seen the Father.

John 14:9

❧

I am God covered with flesh. You have seen the very essence of the Father in Me. He is love.

I am all of the Father that any living human will see. The Father lives in unapproachable light. No one has seen Him or can see Him. I came so mankind could see their God and relate to Him personally. I began walking with My children in the Garden, and I do so yet today. I have never stopped talking to them. I carry the loving and merciful essence of the Father to His children, who are My children.

Enjoy the presence of God in your life! I am here with you, right now in this very moment. In Me, you see the Father who awaits in heaven. Let us complete the journey in anticipation. I will then take you to Him.

DECEMBER 17

I and the Father are one.

John 10:30

༄༅

I am one with the Father. Though separate, we share a common purpose, will, and power. It is a great mystery that man cannot understand.

I am as much God as the Father is. It is the same with the Holy Spirit. Yet, each of Us has a different function in the great plan of redemption in history. The Father is flawlessly righteous. His holiness separates Him from sinful mankind. I am the Son. I engage humanity in all of its sinfulness. The Holy Spirit is the Comforter. He bears witness of Me in the world. Though We share the same essence, We are different persons and manifestations of the same God. Love and mercy and anger and judgment flow from Us.

My Father has a plan for you. I share that plan and work to execute it in the world. The Holy Spirit enables you to understand all I am doing in your life. Each of Us is focused on you.

DECEMBER 18

I am the Alpha and the Omega, the first and
the last, the beginning and the end.

Revelation 22:13

৵৽

I am God. I already was in the beginning and will remain after the end.

Mankind has no concept of eternity. The human mind is bound by time and space and all that is finite. But I am infinite. I have no beginning or end. I am the completeness of all that is. I created the universe, and I will see to its ending. I am the author of salvation and will complete its course through the history of mankind. I am the executor of the Father's plan from its beginning to its ending. As God, I stand over all that was, is, or ever will be.

I am the Alpha and the Omega. You fall within these boundaries. Though you had a beginning, you will have no end. You share an everlasting life with Me.

DECEMBER 19

I am the root and the descendant of
David, the bright morning star.

Revelation 22:16

❧❧

I kept My promise first made in the Garden of Eden. I came
as the Seed of the woman—the One who would crush the
serpent's head. I am from the line of Abraham through
David by way of the flesh. I sit on David's throne forever.

My Word contains the long story of salvation. All that
was promised either has or will come to pass. Though I
came from the line of David, I did not receive the fallen,
sinful nature of mankind that is passed from earthly
fathers to their offspring. Though I came through the flesh
of My mother, My sinless nature came from My sinless
Father. This was the requirement for the sacrifice of the
perfect Lamb so the curse of sin and eternal death would be
broken. I shine as the bright star of the morning, lighting
the sky and heralding the dawn of salvation.

I have given My nature to you. Your sinful nature has
been removed. Only the power of your flesh remains to
hinder your walk. Crucify it daily with Me, and allow it to
die. Let us walk in freedom and victory.

DECEMBER 20

Fear not, I am the first and the last, and the living one. I died, and behold I am alive forevermore, and I have the keys of Death and Hades.

Revelation 1:17-18

ॐ✄

I am the eternal God. My reign is from everlasting to everlasting. Of My kingdom, there is no end. I hold the power over death and hell.

When I died, Satan was sure he had won. Death celebrated and hell rejoiced. When I rose from the grave to live forevermore, everything changed. I conquered death and took away its sting of terror for those who would be My children. To these, I made a way of escaping hell. I paid the penalty in blood for their sin and fulfilled the requirement of the Law. Though they may die physically, those who belong to Me do not suffer the second death in the lake of fire. Instead, they will live eternally with Me in heaven.

I have taken the keys from death and hell. By My authority, I have given you eternal life. Though your earthly shell passes away, death no longer has any authority over you, and hell cannot demand your presence. You belong to Me, and you shall live with Me forevermore.

DECEMBER 21

And to the angel of the church in Thyatira write: 'The words of the Son of God, who has eyes like a flame of fire, and whose feet are like burnished bronze.'

Revelation 2:18

❦

I am the Son of God. I come in authority and might. I look upon evil committed against Me with righteous anger. I will tread upon it with holy feet.

I am jealous for My Church. I gaze at it with eyes of fury. It has wandered after the things of the world. It has left the narrow path to follow after others who are not worthy. Has My bride forgotten who I am? Is she displeased with My wishes for her? Does she want to go her own way? Is error better than My truth or enslavement better than My freedom? A time of purification is coming to My people. My truth is even now being revealed to them so all may see Me as I am. Then, each must decide if they will leave their useless idols and follow where I lead. *What idols do you bow before in this world?*

It is My great desire that you are pure and faithful to Me. Do not become entangled with the world or worship its idols. Nothing good is to be found among them. Take My hand. I will guide you away from them and bring you to safety.

DECEMBER 22

And to the angel of the church in Laodicea
write: 'The words of the Amen, the faithful and
true witness, the beginning of God's creation.'

Revelation 3:14

৵৽

I am the truth. The words I speak are certain. They are a faithful report of all I see as the Creator of all things.

Many of My children will not take My correction. These are stiff-necked and stubborn. The Holy Spirit strives within their hearts, but they will not yield to His convicting work. Some think I am being unfair. Others, that I am too harsh. Some even believe that I ask too much of them. All of these are wrong. I only desire what is best for My children. I have no other agenda. I am not unfair, harsh, or unreasonable. I speak plainly of what I see in their lives and desire that they would change.

Do not harden your heart to My correction. I know who you are becoming, and I see clearly what stands in the way. Let the Holy Spirit do His work in you.

DECEMBER 23

And I, when I am lifted up from the earth,
will draw all people to myself.

John 12:32

❧

The first time I was lifted up, it was in shame and agony. Now when I am lifted up, it is in glory and power.

The cross is a sign of death. Those who were hanged upon them were considered the cursed of mankind. When I was crucified, I became a curse in place of those who would become My children. Through My shame, theirs was removed. Through My agony, they gained the pleasure of heaven. Some of My children have forgotten My words. Though they know how I drew them when I was lifted up before them, they seek to draw others in different ways. Facilities, amenities, music, and marketing have replaced Me as the main draw in much of My Church. I tell you that those who employ such devices labor in vain. It is I who draw people to Myself. When I am faithfully lifted up, I will do the rest.

Do not fall prey to the belief that programs or amenities are the answer. I am the answer. Lift Me up consistently and let Me be the draw. The Holy Spirit will work as I call both the lost and My children to Myself.

DECEMBER 24

My Father is working until now, and I am working.

John 5:17

◈

I am always at work. My Father's plan calls for this to be so.

I am active in the affairs of men. I faithfully move My Father's plan along, keeping it on His schedule. There is no time of rest for Me as I work to build the kingdom one heart at a time. My children need Me to walk with them each day. They must have My guidance so they can remain on their path with Me. They need My encouragement to keep pace with all I am doing. They need My rebuke when they stray. Other things must also be attended to. There are the lost to be found. There are hearts to influence. There are miracles to perform. Though My place is at the right hand of My Father, I walk among mankind doing My Father's work.

I am here with you even now. I revel in your company. You are precious to Me. Your success in your walk is the result of My great work with you. Each day, the fruits of My labors become more apparent. Each day, you become more like Me.

DECEMBER 25

*I am the light of the world. Whoever follows me will
not walk in darkness, but will have the light of life.*

John 8:12

❧

My light shines out into the dark world as a beacon of hope.
I guide those who follow Me, keeping them from the ways of
destruction.

The world is a very dark place. It despises My truth and
seeks to overcome it with the blackness of error. Many have
been led astray in the gray shadows where deception mixes
with truth. My light is pure. It is perfect and sharp. It cuts
deep into the gloom of the hopeless, pointing the way to life.
It does not fade or flicker. Each of My followers can reflect
this light and shine it into the dark to guide the way to Me.
Some shine brightly, while others glow dimly. The brilliance
of their reflected light depends on how closely they embrace
Me and walk in My truth. When taken as a whole, My
Church has great potential to shine in this world. They
need only to allow the Holy Spirit to polish their hearts with
My truth.

I have much light to shine upon you. Allow Me to remove
any falseness that darkens your reflection of My light. *If I
point out the places of darkness in your heart, will you allow
them to be filled with the light of My truth?*

DECEMBER 26

I am the resurrection and the life. Whoever
believes in me, though he die, yet shall he live.

John 11:25

❧

Right now, in this very moment, I am the resurrection and the life. All who believe in Me *already* live forever.

Who among My children are living each day with an eternal perspective? Who among them walks in this reality with Me? Those who are doing so live differently from those who have not grasped the truth of this matter. These see the continuity of their relationship with Me beyond the present. They understand that physical death is but a step along the way in their unending walk with Me. Earthly treasures hold little sway over them. Persecutions and trials lose their terror. All who have My eternal perspective live with Me in the moment. They allow no thoughts of going their own way now and joining back with Me later.

I have given you eternal life. You possess it in all of its fullness. Adopt an eternal perspective of your life. Walk closely with Me, and get to know Me as I am. Do not wait until this life is at an end. Do it while it is yet *today*.

DECEMBER 27

*I am the bread of life; whoever comes to me shall not
hunger, and whoever believes in me shall never thirst.*

John 6:35

❧

Only I can satisfy your true hunger. Only I can make you
full.

Everyone has a hunger driving them to find satisfaction.
Yet, most do not know what they hunger for. They run from
this to that, sampling what the world offers along the way.
They fill themselves here and there, but it does not last. It
is never enough. I am the only food that satisfies because
the hunger is spiritual. The world offers nothing that can
satisfy. Its best good will not, nor will its worst evil. Those
who partake of the world come away empty though they
have gorged themselves to the full. The wise among My
children have ceased chasing after what can never satisfy.
They no longer look to the world for their fulfillment. They
have Me. I am enough.

Temporal things only fill you temporarily. Eternal things
satisfy you eternally. Run to Me. Have your fill. I offer an
endless supply to all who ask. Love, mercy, understanding,
forgiveness, kindness, and truth await. I can satisfy your
every need.

DECEMBER 28

Truly, truly, I say to you, I am the door of the sheep.

John 10:7

❧

I stand between My children and the enemy. No one may join My Church without coming through Me.

Every religion has its own rites of membership. These are the doors through which each must pass to join the group as a member. I am the door to My Church. No one can join with My sheep unless they come through Me. My Church is not a club as many have come to believe. It is more than an occasional social gathering. It does not begin and end with a creed shared among the flock. My Church is My Body. It is living and breathing, moving and adapting. All who belong are knit together by the Holy Spirit. These walk in union together under My control.

You are one of My children. You have entered this fellowship through Me. I stand between you and the enemy who seeks to join us in falseness. Stay with Me and remain under My protection.

December 29

I am the good shepherd. The good shepherd
lays down his life for the sheep.

John 10:11

❧

I know My sheep and they know Me. They follow the sound of My voice. It is the voice of truth in their ears.

I allow My sheep to be gathered together under shepherds I have called to share in My work. The hearts of these leaders belong to Me. They hear My voice clearly and lead My sheep in truth and love. I partition My flock and send them to these shepherds so they may be fed and nurtured in My ways. However, many of My sheep have not heeded My voice. They have gone their own way and joined themselves to hirelings instead of My shepherds. Hirelings do not love My sheep. They use them for their own purposes. They allow wolves to creep in among My sheep, putting them in danger. While My shepherds follow My example and lay down their lives for My sheep, hirelings keep their lives for themselves. Their ways are false because they are false. All who join themselves to such people do so at their own peril. *Let all of My sheep hear these words!*

Do not run after hirelings who tickle your ears with words that appeal to your pride and your flesh. Stay with Me and those shepherds I have appointed for you. Let the words of truth sound in your ears and guide you along the way. You will be kept from much harm.

DECEMBER 30

I am the true vine, and my Father is the vinedresser.

John 15:1

❧❦

I am the vine from which all of My children in the vineyard grow. My Father watches over each branch with loving carefulness. He waits to see the amount of fruit they will bear for the kingdom.

All that My children need is found in Me. My resources are boundless and come from the goodness of My Father. All who grow in Me have access to these resources. They are fed and watered as needed, gaining strength from My supernatural power. Every good branch in the vineyard shares a common purpose. It is to bear much fruit in Me and bring glory to My Father. In the end, the fruit of all will be weighed and rewards handed out. The fruitful branches will receive much.

It is My wish that you would be fruitful. Abide in Me and feed from My supernatural resources. Let your every effort be toward growth in Me so you may bear much fruit.

DECEMBER 31

I am, and you will see the Son of Man seated at the right hand of Power, and coming with the clouds of heaven.

Mark 14:62

৵৽

The right-hand seat is the place of honor. Because of My obedience, My Father has exalted Me in His presence and given Me this seat.

When My work in history is finished, I will sit down. I sat after the great work of redemption was accomplished, and I will sit when the work of salvation is complete. All flesh shall see Me at My return. My creation will rejoice that its time of redemption has fully come. My children who are living at the time will rejoice in My presence. But the wicked will quake before Me. Their hearts will melt when they behold My face. Though they have shaken their fists at Me, yet they will bend their knee. Even so, they will not find reprieve from My wrath. On that day, the longsuffering of God will come to an end, and justice will be meted out upon the guilty.

You will be with Me on that great and terrible day. Your heart will be full of My love and bursting with joy. You will see the fulfillment of My love and My wrath. You will bend your knee before your King.

SCRIPTURE LOCATOR

Scripture cross-reference by day.

Matthew

Matt 4:4	June 20	Matt 7:3-5	October 2
Matt 4:7	June 21	Matt 7:6	October 5
Matt 4:10	June 22	Matt 7:13	April 18
Matt 4:17	July 7	Matt 7:14	April 19
Matt 5:3	May 1	Matt 7:15	June 25
Matt 5:4	May 2	Matt 7:16	June 27
Matt 5:5	May 3	Matt 7:17-18	August 7
Matt 5:6	May 4	Matt 7:20	August 8
Matt 5:7	May 5	Matt 7:21	August 10
Matt 5:8	May 6	Matt 7:22	August 11
Matt 5:9	May 7	Matt 7:23	August 12
Matt 5:13	May 12	Matt 7:24-25	November 18
Matt 5:14-16	May 13	Matt 8:11	March 15
Matt 5:17	December 14	Matt 8:32	June 13
Matt 5:21-22	May 14	Matt 9:9	July 1
Matt 5:23-24	May 15	Matt 9:12-13	October 10
Matt 5:27-28	May 16	Matt 9:22	February 27
Matt 5:29-30	May 17	Matt 10:8	June 5
Matt 5:33-37	May 18	Matt 10:16	September 14
Matt 5:38-39	May 19	Matt 10:24-25	September 1
Matt 5:40-41	May 20	Matt 10:35-36	July 17
Matt 5:42	May 21	Matt 10:37	July 18
Matt 5:47	May 26	Matt 10:41-42	August 26
Matt 5:48	May 31	Matt 11:11	March 12
Matt 6:1	October 9	Matt 11:12	March 13
Matt 6:5	February 16	Matt 11:16-17	September 15
Matt 6:6	February 17	Matt 11:18-19	September 16
Matt 6:7	February 18	Matt 11:25	October 30
Matt 6:8	February 19	Matt 11:28	July 10
Matt 6:9	February 9	Matt 11:29-30	July 11
Matt 6:10	February 10	Matt 12:8	December 8
Matt 6:11	February 11	Matt 12:25-26	June 9
Matt 6:12	February 12	Matt 12:28	June 10
Matt 6:13	February 13	Matt 12:30	June 28
Matt 6:19	August 20	Matt 12:34-35	August 9
Matt 6:20	August 21	Matt 13:3	August 15
Matt 6:33	November 7	Matt 13:19	August 16
Matt 7:1-2	October 1	Matt 13:20-21	August 17

Matt 13:22	August 18	Matt 21:42	December 13
Matt 13:23	August 19	Matt 21:44	July 8
Matt 13:24-26	March 26	Matt 22:14	July 9
Matt 13:31-32	March 14	Matt 22:21	July 22
Matt 13:33	March 16	Matt 22:37-38	July 23
Matt 13:38	March 27	Matt 22:39	July 24
Matt 13:41-42	March 28	Matt 22:42	January 4
Matt 13:43	March 29	Matt 23:2-3	October 17
Matt 13:44	March 17	Matt 23:4	October 18
Matt 13:45-46	March 18	Matt 23:5-7	October 19
Matt 13:47-48	March 19	Matt 23:15	October 20
Matt 14:31	February 23	Matt 23:23-24	October 21
Matt 15:7-9	October 13	Matt 23:27-28	October 22
Matt 15:14	October 29	Matt 24:4	September 17
Matt 16:3	October 27	Matt 24:6-8	September 18
Matt 16:23a	June 16	Matt 24:10	September 19
Matt 16:23b	June 17	Matt 24:11	September 21
Matt 18:3	April 16	Matt 24:12	September 20
Matt 18:10	November 12	Matt 24:24	June 26
Matt 18:19-20	February 15	Matt 25:1-4	March 23
Matt 18:22	July 20	Matt 25:5	March 24
Matt 19:23	March 9	Matt 25:10-12	March 25
Matt 19:24	March 10	Matt 25:21	August 30
Matt 19:29	August 28	Matt 25:40	July 25
Matt 20:1-7	March 20	Matt 25:41	June 1
Matt 20:8-12	March 21	Matt 28:18	December 3
Matt 20:13-15	March 22		

Mark

Mark 1:15	March 2	Mark 8:12	January 22
Mark 2:9-11	December 4	Mark 8:21	January 13
Mark 2:27	October 23	Mark 9:23	February 22
Mark 3:27	June 11	Mark 9:25	June 3
Mark 4:24-25	November 10	Mark 9:29	June 12
Mark 4:26-27	March 30	Mark 9:33	January 2
Mark 4:28-29	March 31	Mark 9:35	July 15
Mark 4:39	December 5	Mark 9:40	June 14
Mark 5:19	November 28	Mark 10:14	March 8
Mark 6:4	November 11	Mark 10:15	March 7
Mark 6:31	July 26	Mark 10:21	July 16
Mark 6:38	January 12	Mark 10:24	March 6
Mark 7:29	February 26	Mark 10:31	March 11

Mark 10:36	January 8	Mark 12:34	March 5
Mark 10:42-44	July 21	Mark 12:43-44	September 12
Mark 10:52	February 25	Mark 13:31	December 12
Mark 11:17	February 28	Mark 13:37	July 19
Mark 11:22	February 29	Mark 14:38	November 22
Mark 11:24	February 7	Mark 14:62	December 31
Mark 12:24	October 28		

Luke

Luke 5:4	November 16	Luke 10:16	September 28
Luke 5:10	July 12	Luke 10:18	June 6
Luke 5:36	October 24	Luke 10:19	June 7
Luke 5:37-38	October 25	Luke 10:20	June 8
Luke 5:39	October 26	Luke 10:22	December 2
Luke 6:22	May 8	Luke 10:41-42	November 13
Luke 6:23	May 9	Luke 11:9	February 1
Luke 6:24-25	May 10	Luke 11:10	February 4
Luke 6:26	May 11	Luke 11:13	February 5
Luke 6:27-28	September 29	Luke 11:39	October 12
Luke 6:31	May 22	Luke 12:1	October 15
Luke 6:32	May 23	Luke 12:2	October 16
Luke 6:33	May 24	Luke 12:4-5	September 9
Luke 6:34	May 25	Luke 12:6-7	September 10
Luke 6:35a	May 27	Luke 12:15	November 14
Luke 6:35b	May 28	Luke 12:32	August 24
Luke 6:35c	May 29	Luke 12:33	August 25
Luke 6:36	May 30	Luke 12:34	August 22
Luke 6:39	January 21	Luke 12:49	December 15
Luke 6:40	July 13	Luke 12:51	January 24
Luke 6:46	January 28	Luke 12:57	January 20
Luke 7:40	November 8	Luke 13:6-7	August 13
Luke 7:47	October 11	Luke 13:8-9	August 14
Luke 8:25	January 15	Luke 13:24	April 17
Luke 8:30	June 2	Luke 13:29-30	August 31
Luke 8:50	February 24	Luke 14:3	January 23
Luke 9:18	January 5	Luke 14:28-30	July 2
Luke 9:20	January 6	Luke 14:33	July 6
Luke 9:23	July 3	Luke 16:13	August 23
Luke 9:24-25	July 4	Luke 16:15	October 8
Luke 9:58	July 14	Luke 17:3-4	October 4
Luke 9:62	July 5	Luke 17:6	February 3
Luke 10:3	June 24	Luke 17:20	March 3

Luke 17:21	March 4	Luke 20:38	November 9
Luke 17:26	November 27	Luke 21:12	September 23
Luke 18:7	January 25	Luke 21:13	September 24
Luke 18:8	January 26	Luke 21:14-15	September 26
Luke 18:11	February 20	Luke 22:31	June 18
Luke 18:13	February 21	Luke 22:35	January 11
Luke 18:27	November 15	Luke 22:46	June 19
Luke 18:32	September 2	Luke 22:53	June 23
Luke 19:10	April 30	Luke 24:38	January 10
Luke 19:40	December 6		

John

John 1:38	January 1	John 6:63	April 15
John 3:3	April 11	John 6:67	January 19
John 3:5-6	April 13	John 7:24	October 6
John 3:7	April 12	John 8:7	October 3
John 3:8	April 14	John 8:12	December 25
John 3:16a	April 1	John 8:31-32	November 5
John 3:16b	April 2	John 8:44	June 29
John 3:16c	April 3	John 8:58	December 1
John 3:17a	April 4	John 9:35	January 7
John 3:17b	April 5	John 10:7	December 28
John 3:18a	April 6	John 10:9	April 20
John 3:18b	April 7	John 10:10	June 4
John 3:19	April 8	John 10:11	December 29
John 3:20	April 9	John 10:16	November 26
John 3:21	April 10	John 10:17-18	December 7
John 4:34	November 23	John 10:27	June 30
John 4:38	July 28	John 10:30	December 17
John 5:14	June 15	John 11:25	December 26
John 5:17	December 24	John 11:39	November 17
John 5:21	December 11	John 11:40	January 14
John 5:30	October 7	John 11:43	December 10
John 5:39-40	April 29	John 12:24	July 29
John 5:44	January 16	John 12:32	December 23
John 6:5	January 9	John 13:10	November 6
John 6:20	November 24	John 13:12	January 29
John 6:35	December 27	John 13:34-35	July 27
John 6:37	April 27	John 13:38	January 31
John 6:40	April 28	John 14:2	August 29
John 6:46	November 25	John 14:6a	April 21
John 6:61	January 18	John 14:6b	April 22

John 14:6c	April 23	John 15:20	September 5
John 14:6d	April 24	John 15:21	September 6
John 14:9	December 16	John 15:27	September 25
John 14:12	November 2	John 16:2	September 22
John 14:13	February 8	John 16:12	October 31
John 14:14	February 2	John 16:14	February 6
John 14:19	November 30	John 16:23	February 14
John 14:23-24	July 30	John 16:33	September 30
John 14:27	September 13	John 17:2	April 25
John 15:1	December 30	John 17:3	April 26
John 15:2	August 2	John 17:15	September 8
John 15:5	August 1	John 17:18	September 7
John 15:6	August 3	John 17:20-21	November 4
John 15:8	August 5	John 18:4	January 3
John 15:11	August 6	John 18:36	March 1
John 15:14-15	November 29	John 20:29	January 17
John 15:16	August 4	John 21:5	January 27
John 15:18	September 3	John 21:6	December 9
John 15:19	September 4	John 21:15	January 30

Acts

| Acts 9:15-16 | September 11 | Acts 20:35 | November 3 |
| Acts 18:9-10 | September 27 | Acts 26:16 | November 1 |

Revelation

Rev 1:17-18	December 20	Rev 3:19	November 20
Rev 2:4	November 19	Rev 3:20	November 21
Rev 2:18	December 21	Rev 22:12	August 27
Rev 3:1	October 14	Rev 22:13	December 18
Rev 3:14	December 22	Rev 22:16	December 19

ADDITIONAL PUBLICATIONS

Jesus in Disguise

Where are the Men?
The Journey to Discipleship in Jesus

History Hunters Series
*Historical mysteries for middle schoolers
and young adults*

Made in the USA
Columbia, SC
09 May 2021